Bloody Marys

Sanguine Solutions
for a Slew of Situations

Recipes and Revelries by
Judy Bennett

Camarilla Books
Portland, Oregon

Bloody Marys: Sanguine Solutions for a Slew of Situations
by Judy Bennett

Published by Camarilla Books
5132 SW Richenberg Ct. Portland, OR 97239
www.bloodymarybook.com

Cover and interior design: Bo Björn Johnson
Editing: Linda M. Meyer
Illustrations: Andrew Zubko (www.zubko.com)

Printed in the U.S.A.

9 8 7 6 5 4 3 2 1

ISBN: 978-0-61547-104-4

After a couple Bloody Marys, you're almost cute.

One day I woke up with the worst hangover you ever saw. Ordinarily I'd mix m'self up a good strong Bloody Mary to set things to rights. Only on this partikler day, I didn't have no vodka in the house or tomato juice or nothin', but I recollect I heard somewheres that breathin' pure oxygen is good for a swole head. So I started thinkin', my buddy Frank is on oxygen cuz he done smoked for better 'n sixty years, mebbe I'll run over t' his house and get a snort. Well, I got as far as the garage when I seen my acetylene torch sittin' by the workbench. I thought to myself, why, I got no need to go over t' Frank's when there's perfectly good oxygen right here. So I bent over, give that ol' valve a twist, and blammo! My cheeks was flapping like a dog with its head out the car winder. I couldn't get my eyelids down for about an hour and a half. Tell the truth, it didn't do a hell of a lot for my hangover, neither. Next time I'm makin' me a Bloody Mary, that's for damn sure.

—*Arnie, VA Medical Center, Room 208*

Hey, dummy! See if the nurse will make you one—O negative. *Hahahahahaha...*

    —*Hazel, Arnie's wife (with a fresh Bloody Mary in hand)*

Acknowledgments

B efore we get started, I'd just like to lift my glass to some great people.

This book absolutely would not have happened without the trust and support of my friends and family. A very special thank you goes to Jean Ann van Krevelen, whose valuable marketing assistance finally got me off my caboose. I also want to thank Jen Weaver-Neist, Linda Meyer, Allison Collins, and all the lovely ladies of WiPP (Women in Portland Publishing) for loving the idea from the get-go and for taking a leap of faith with me; Andy Zubko for the kicky glass illustrations; Bo Bjorn Johnson for spinning straw into gold; Kara Newman of *Spice & Ice*; all my new LUPEC buddies for their generous technical assistance; the always effervescent Women With Moxie; and Alicia Davenport for not letting me wimp out. My deep appreciation goes to everyone who contributed material: Dave and Cyndi Hyde, Patty Earley, Bev Fagan, Alex Lieber, Marie Dietrich, Suzanne Mauget, Troy Itami, Alisa Sloan, Ezra Johnson-Greenough, Chris Lindland, Tori Harms, Karen Hochman, Juliana Gonzales, and Bobbie Weiner. Thanks also to my tasting team: Kristin Erdmann, Jessica Glenn, Rebecca and Kat at Portland Spa, Manoah Mahanraj, Mark and Shari Williams, Siobhan Caverly, and Gene Koenig. And my deepest gratitude goes to Tom, *il mio accomplice*, for taking "hottie" to A Whole Nother Level.

Thank you, one and all, for hopping on my little Mary-Go-Round. It's been a fun ride.

Contents

Disclaimer (The Lawyers Made Me Say This) . . . xi

Introduction . . . xiii

Important Bartender-y Facts . . . xv
    Measurements . . . xvi
    More Ice Advice . . . xvi
    Types of Glasses . . . xviii
    Common Terms . . . xx
    Other Tips . . . xxi
    Helpful Resources . . . xxiii

About the Photographs . . . xxv

PART I - CELEBRATIONS
Bloody Marys for Everyday Victories

    Let Me Be the First to Welcome You to the Neighborhood
        (Petiot's Original Bloody Mary) . . . 2
    It Took Me All Friggin' Weekend,
        But I Finally Got the Grout Clean . . . 8
    Tonight's Our Anniversary and My Mom's Watching the Kids . . . 12
    The Pregnancy Test Was Negative . . . 16
    Tell Us Again How He Proposed
        (Hemingway's Perfect Bloody Mary) . . . 20
    I Landed the Account, Bitchez . . . 24
    My Daughter's New Boyfriend Isn't an Asswipe . . . 28
    Garnish: The Bloody Paparazzi . . . 32

PART II - INCANTATIONS

Bloody Marys for Bedazzlement

Maybe They Won't Notice I Burned the Steaks . . . 36

The Way to a Man's Heart Is Through His Stomach,
But That's Not Where I'm Headed . . . 40

Remind Me Why I'm Going Skydiving Tomorrow . . . 46

When I Win the Lottery, I'm Quitting This Crappy Job . . . 50

I Know We Just Met, But I Want to Have Your Babies . . . 54

I Want This Promotion So Bad I Can Taste It . . . 58

I Really Hope I Fit In at This New Country Club . . . 62

Go Packers . . . 68

Garnish: I Know What You Drank Last Summer . . . 71

PART III - CONFLAGRATIONS

Bloody Marys for Settling the Score

He Called Out My Sister's Name In Bed . . . 74

They Told Me It Was a Costume Party . . . 78

If You Think I'm Paying for This Haircut,
You're Sadly Mistaken . . . 82

I Oughta Put a Big Carbon Footprint Right On Your Face,
You SUV-Driving, Animal-Eating, Plastic-Wrapped,
High-Fructose Son of a Bitch . . . 88

My Kids Found My "Private Drawer" . . . 92

Garnish: The Bloody Mary Hall of Flame . . . 96

PART IV - AFFIRMATIONS

Bloody Marys for Hedonism

It's My Birthday and I Want Breakfast in Bed . . . 100

This Outfit and I Deserve a Night on the Town . . . 104

This Is My First Really Healthy Relationship . . . 108

My High School Reunion is Five Pounds and Two Weeks Away . . . 112

Hos Before Bros . . . 116

The More Resentment I Release, the More Love I Can Express . . . 120

Garnish: Will the Real Bloody Mary Please Stand Up? . . . 124

PART V - DESTINATIONS

Bloody Marys for Tastebud Odysseys

My Tax Refund Just Bought Me a Week in Cabo . . . 130

Actually, I'm More of a Ski Lodge Bum . . . 134

I've Decided to Go Back to College . . . 138

I Never Got to Go Backpacking Through Europe . . . 142

We Should Go to Hawaii More Often . . . 146

What a Perfect Day for a Picnic . . . 150

What's the Guatemalan Phrase for "Please Untie Me" . . . 154

I Spent Three Months in Palm Desert One Weekend . . . 158

Garnish: Location, Location, Location . . . 162

PART VI - TRANSFORMATIONS

Bloody Marys for Rites of Passage

We Need a Bigger Garage . . . 164
All I Need Is Comfort Food and a Little "Me" Time . . . 168
Good Help Is So Hard to Find . . . 172
Blondes May Have More Fun,
    But Brunettes Have Better Fun . . . 178
I Need a Hobby Now That the Kids Have Left Home . . . 184
Garnish: The Bartender's Friend: A Glossary . . . 189

PART VII - COMMISERATIONS

Bloody Marys for Pity Parties

It's Not You, It's Me . . . 192
I Can't Manage My Money If I Don't Have Any . . . 196
There's Nothing Fun to Do This Weekend . . . 200
It's Raining for the 47th Day in a Row . . . 204
I Haven't Had a Cold This Bad in Years . . . 208

Epilogue . . . 213
    I Think I'm Turning into My Mother . . . 214

Recipe References . . . 217
About the Author . . . 222

Disclaimer

(The Lawyers Made Me Say This)

A few scenarios described in this book involve enjoying your Bloody Mary solo. I am not, however, suggesting that habitually drinking alone is a healthy way of life. Neither am I recommending alcohol as a way to solve your problems. If we have learned anything from the sixties, or from Lindsay Lohan in the noughties, it's that common sense and responsible moderation should prevail in your alcohol-quaffing activities. A few other rules before we get started: (1) Do not operate heavy machinery—not even a blow dryer—or drive a car while under the influence of this book or its contents. (2) No drunk-dialing, period. It just never ends well. (3) While the information contained in the following pages will make you more urbane, better looking, smarter, and a more conscientious parent, it will not help your dancing, karaoke-singing, or sexual abilities. (4) If you suspect you might be pregnant, are under age, or both, please give this book to someone who can enjoy it.

Introduction

Picking up a cocktail book by an unknown author may be a lot like being the first person ever to see a cow. He looked at it from every angle, cocked his head, and said to himself, "I don't know what's gonna come out of here, but whatever it is, I'm gonna drink it!"

Your curiosity will not go unrewarded, brave soul. Luckily, what you will find in this book is something far more interesting than milk. You're about to experience forty-five of the most luscious and culturally diverse Bloody Marys on the planet. Why Bloody Marys? Come on. Anyone can pour wine into a glass and pronounce it "eviscerated" or "*pétillant*," but who else besides Mary can inspire a whole dossier? She can be coy and flirtatious or completely inscrutable. She can shake her moneymaker in your face. She can sing you to sleep or slap you awake. You think a milkshake brings boys to the yard? Puh-lease.

By now you're probably asking yourself, "With so many versions to choose from, which one should I serve at my next party?" Easy. The most effective way to use this book is to match your mood and/or event to one of the drink headings found in the table of contents, flip to that page, and revel in the description of that drink's particular nuances as well as the tips on how to showcase your creation. Another way, if you're so inclined, is to start at the beginning, make and sample every recipe, and bookmark your special favorites. No matter if that next party is a baptism or a booty call, there is a Mary that will be just what you're looking for. I will introduce you to Bloody Marys for every stage of your life, whether you are just learning your way around the post-collegiate world, newly married, navigating through middle age with or without children, or sashaying into retirement. The situations described won't all apply to you right this minute, but they will someday. Or they may remind you of women you know. A seasoned hostess knows that choosing a beverage for the bash isn't just about food pairings; it's about understanding your guests and the mood you are trying to set, plus showing a little creative flair in the bargain. This book will give you that seasoning. What, no guests? Not a problem. There are recipes here that suit solo scenarios, too. But the recipes are only the beginning. This book also dishes dirt about the Bloody Mary's checkered past, and introduces the cultural icons and urban legends inspired by her. Don't miss the Bloody Mary Hall of Flame, the wackiest concoctions ever. For happy hour brownie points, there is a Bloody Mary glossary. You'll learn what Mary fans put in their glasses in different parts of the world, and the surprising medicinal and sexual benefits of Tabasco and lime. What you are holding in your hands is a backstage pass to the Bloody Mary comeback tour.

So what do you say? Actually, I'll tell you what to say. Say "so long" to so-so soirées. Bloody Marys offer a sanguine solution to any situation—and how can milk compete with that?

Important Bartender-y Facts

H ere are some basic measurements and mixing terms you'll want to know to help you accurately recreate the recipes in this book. Fumbling around unprepared is all well and fine for teenagers at the drive-in, but you'll get better results and have more fun if you start out with the right information. Once you have the terminology down, you should familiarize yourself with the necessary supplies. You will need:

* a set of measuring spoons

* a shot glass with 1-, 1½-, and 2-ounce demarcations

* a 4-cup measuring cup

* a cocktail shaker

* a strainer (if your shaker doesn't already come equipped with one)

* a few wooden or plastic skewers

It's also handy to have access to an icemaker, but if you don't, fill your ice cube trays pronto, or stop at the store and buy a bagful. I've also included an illustrated guide showing the various kinds of glassware you'll encounter throughout the book.

There! You should be all set now. Ready to get started?

MEASUREMENTS

You should always create your drinks according to your own tastes and mood—Mary would expect nothing less! The measurements displayed on the right are approximations that work for me when I'm mixing my Marys, but feel free to experiment with what works best for you.

MORE ICE ADVICE

Always try to use the biggest pieces of ice you can get away with. The smaller the cubes, the faster they'll melt and dilute the flavors you've worked so hard to create. Crushed ice, acceptable when used for building a drink, can give Bloody Marys a fun, slushy texture; however, be warned that they do melt the quickest. Save them for small servings that you can consume fairly fast. Cubed ice is almost never a wrong choice. It's even better when the cubes have been in the icemaker bin for a while and have congealed into one giant iceberg. You can then put the glacier in your (clean) sink and chip away the biggest chunks that will fit in your glass. And for party planning, a good rule of thumb is one pound of ice per person.

1/4 cup	2 ounces
1/3 cup	3 ounces
1/2 cup	4 ounces
2/3 cup	5 ounces
3/4 cup	6 ounces
1 cup	8 ounces
1 pint	16 ounces
1 quart	32 ounces
750 ml bottle	25.4 ounces
1 liter bottle	33.8 ounces
1 medium lemon	3 Tablespoons juice
1 medium lime	2 Tablespoons juice
Dash	1/32 ounce *(So don't get carried away!)*
Fifth	25.6 ounces (about 17 jiggers)
Finger	the actual thickness of one of your fingers *(My index finger measures not quite 3/4 of an inch.)*
Jigger	1½ ounces or 3 Tablespoons
Part	the proportion of one ingredient in relation to the total volume *(Sorry, I don't divulge the thicknesses of my other parts.)*
Shot	1 ounce or 2 Tablespoons
Splash	1/8 ounce

TYPES OF GLASSES

When serving your lovingly handcrafted Bloody Mary, you will want to use the right type of glassware to present it in its best light. (The term "glassware" comes from an ancient Etruscan word meaning, "Has anybody seen my drink?") Nowadays, there are many types of glasses that are appropriate to use for Bloody Marys, depending on the serving size and social setting. Here are examples of the glassware I recommend to accompany the recipes in this book.

Collins

Flask

Highball

Hurricane

Martini

Mug

Old Fashioned

Pilsner

Pint

Pitcher

Punchbowl

Shot

COMMON TERMS

Boxing: Pouring liquid into and out of a cocktail shaker just once, to combine the ingredients. This is used when vigorously shaking your Bloody Mary isn't necessary, or if your guests are too impatient to wait while you prepare their drinks in a more theatrical fashion.

Building: To add ingredients directly to the glass your Bloody Mary will be consumed in. You can then stir the drink with a long-handled spoon, a swizzle stick, a stalk of celery, or a clean index finger.

Rimming: This is easy to master, and your guests will appreciate your thoughtfulness for going the extra mile. (Besides, it's sort of fun once you get the hang of it.) Here's how to do it: wet the edge of the glass by rubbing a piece of citrus fruit around it. Limes tend to work better than lemons because of the higher sugar content in limes—the stickier the juice, the more impressive the results. Spread a thin layer of salt (or whatever dry ingredient you're using) on a small plate. Holding the glass upside down, roll the moistened rim through the salt until evenly coated. With a little practice, you'll be rimming like a pro in no time.

Shaking: To simultaneously chill and mix the drink ingredients before serving. Fill your shaker 3/4 full of ice cubes, add the Bloody Mary ingredients, and tightly affix the lid. Do not use crushed ice, as it will clog up the strainer and make things more difficult than they need to be. Holding the shaker in both hands, give it several sharp, snappy shakes. (As the evening wears on, it's fun to have your guests read that sentence three times as fast as they can.) You can stop shaking when condensation begins to form on the surface of the shaker. I recommend shaking a Bloody Mary more than any other method of mixing; it's a fantastic way to tone your upper arms.

Straining: The muscle fatigue that results from exuberant shaking. Not only that, but straining is also a technique that allows you to neatly pour a drink into your glass while leaving the ice behind. If you want to serve your Bloody Mary over ice, use fresh ice cubes and discard the ones that were in the shaker. I'm not sure what difference it makes, frankly, but that's what all the experts advise. Just tell people I said so, and leave it at that.

OTHER TIPS I'VE LEARNED ALONG THE WAY

The Fresh vs. Prepared Debate: I like shortcuts as much as the next girl, but there are times when only the real McCoy will suffice. For example, under normal circumstances, if someone has gone to the trouble to put lemon juice in a bottle for me, it just seems impolite to squeeze my own. But if it's a Special Occasion and my aim is to impress, you bet your bippy I'm going to be cutting up some lemons. My advice to you is to let your conscience, your time frame, and your skill level with a knife be your guide. If your friends are that judgmental, they can jolly well go drink someplace else.

Top-of-the-Line Ingredients vs. Generic: I consulted the experts on this point. Some say that the finest ingredients will yield the finest results. Makes a certain amount of sense, doesn't it? But then others told me that if, for instance, your tomato juice is on the blah side, your spices get a chance to stand out more. Sort of like putting a bright orange couch in an all-white room. And that brings me to the vodka debate. Everyone wants to know why, if vodka is odorless and tasteless, there are so many opinions about which one is the best. All the bartenders and distillers I consulted agree that there is a difference in the way plain unflavored vodka tastes, depending on what's in it and how it was made. Again, it's ultimately up to you and the effect you're trying to create. Sometimes I recommend buying the best quality you can afford, but it doesn't matter in all cases. The same holds true with rum, tequila, gin, and beer (at least in the recipes in this book).

Tabasco vs. "Other" Hot Sauces: In the ethnic or specialty food aisle of the grocery store, there may be four dozen kinds of hot sauce with cute names like Dave's Ultimate Insanity, Ow! Say Tongue, Ass Blaster, Slap Your Mama, Lethal Ingestion, and so on. Tabasco sauce is just one type that's very easy to find, isn't killer hot, and is universally known. While I may name one or the other with the recipes in this book, feel free to use whatever fries your fanny!

What to Do if You Go Overboard with the Hot Sauce: Instinct will make you reach for a glass of ice water. Don't. It will bring temporary relief while the water is in your mouth, but it will ultimately make matters worse. Keep some bread or pieces of cheese handy. Bread helps soak up the capsaicin and moves it on down your digestive tract where it becomes another problem entirely. Dairy products coat your tongue and mucous membranes, allowing the hot sauce to pass through your system with less detrimental impact. A word about handling chiles: it's best to wear gloves for this task, or at least wash your hands thoroughly afterward. Otherwise, next thing you know, you'll rub your eyes or some other sensitive area where the bread and cheese trick will have no effect. All you can do at that point is apply cold water, wait, and pray. I can tell you from experience that running around the kitchen, flapping your arms and shrieking is no help at all.

HELPFUL RESOURCES
Garnishes

* **Country Mercantile Inc.** (www.countrymercan tile.com)—a smorgasbord of pickled delights. Mushrooms, garlic, asparagus, okra, beans, carrots...one-stop shopping for Bloody Mary garnishes.

* **CyberCucina** (www.cybercucina.com)—for any type of olive your heart or tummy desires. There were some I hadn't even heard of before.

Hot Sauces and Bloody Mary Mixes

* **The Best Hot Sauce** (www.the-best-hot-sauce. com)—more varieties of Bloody Mary mix than I've seen anywhere, ranging from Bacon Cheeseburger flavor and burn-your-gizzard hot to all natural. They have hot sauces, too, arranged by country. You'll also find garnishes, rubs, marinades, salsas, recipes, and more, more, more!

* **FireGirl, Inc.** (www.firegirl.com)—purveyors of a stunning array of hot sauces. Don't miss their Woman Power and Sexual Innuendo categories. The descriptions alone are worth a visit to the site.

* **PepperFool** (www.pepperfool.com)—handy links for sourcing fresh, dried, or powdered chiles. Browse through the vast selection, and spend some time educating yourself about different chiles and where they come from, while you're at it.

* **Tabasco Country Store** (www.countrystore.tabas
  co.com)—Tabasco sauce has been a trusted kitch-
  en staple for decades, and now you can finally
  order it by the gallon. See all the flavors here.

* **McClure's** (www.mcclurespickles.com/products)
  makes just about the best ready-made mix I've
  run into anywhere, but you'd better make sure
  you like pickles before you try it. Just sayin'.

Vodkas

* **Bakon Vodka** (www.bakonvodka.com)—savory,
  homemade goodness without the fuss. The taste is
  so authentic, you can almost hear it sizzle.

* **Crop Harvest Earth Co.** (www.cropvodka.
  com)—organic vodka varieties. If your local
  boozatorium doesn't carry tomato- or cucumber-
  flavored vodka, you can order it here. You won't
  be sorry you did.

* **Northwest Distillery** (www.nwdistillery.com)—
  home of fine, handcrafted Oregon spirits, it is
  also the home of the enchanting Meghan Zonich.
  Well, not really, but she and her hubby work there
  creating vodka that was awarded a bronze medal
  at the San Francisco World Spirits competition
  and a silver medal at the International Spirits
  competition in London. Pick up a bottle of their
  "Liquid" vodka and your liquor cabinet will be
  forever in your debt.

About the Photographs

Most of this book's snapshots came into my possession when my parents moved from their home to an assisted living facility. Had I gotten my hands on them sooner, I would have been able to find out the names and relationships of the people in the photographs. Unfortunately, my parents' dementia was pretty far advanced by then, so lots of these smiling folks are strangers to me too. The few pictures that didn't come out of those crumbling scrapbooks were bought from second-hand stores around northwestern Oregon. (But seriously, people! Who gives away family photos to junk shops??? Uh, I mean, thanks.)

Just as this book revives an icon of yesteryear, I wanted to give the two most important ladies in my life a chance to be vivacious again. One is my mother; the other is her sister, Marie, who was my nanny and later my confidante. They grew up during the Depression in rural South Dakota. My aunt quit school in the sixth grade to raise her younger siblings, including my mom. As soon as she could, Marie shook the farm dust off her shoes and went on to marry a succession of well-to-do men. Five husbands in all, but no children. My mother enlisted in the navy but was soon discharged so she could provide full-time care for her mother, who had fallen ill. She married once, well into her thirties, and I came along the summer she turned forty. Her mother had just passed away a few months before. That was when Marie glided into our lives. My parents had decided to start a business, and they needed someone to care for me.

I didn't fully appreciate it at the time, but I was very lucky

to have two such disparate mommies. My birth mommy was custodial, very proper, and placed high importance on manners and refinement. She nurtured my interest in all things aesthetic and made sure I had a first-rate education. To this very day, we share a love of music and fabulous shoes. By contrast, Marie-mommy was a hell-raiser and an unabashed professional alimony-collector. I learned my numbers, colors, and shapes by dealing hands of five-card draw for her and her friends. By the time I was three, I knew how to pour beer against the side of the glass to keep it from foaming up too much, how to shuffle ball change without falling off the piano, and the meaning of the phrase "no money, no honey." When I was chosen to give the baccalaureate speech at my graduation, I told my mom. When I lost my virginity, I told Marie.

Each of these amazing women added unique ingredients to my personality, and as with Bloody Marys, an ounce or two in either direction would have made me a completely different person. That's why I chose my two moms to represent this book. Plus, I wanted the world to know them the way I think of them, when they were both in their heyday—classy, brassy, wonderful, and wise. Genevieve and Marie, here's to you.

PART I

Celebrations

How to Make Glitter Salt

*Mix a few drops of food coloring into kosher (not iodized!) salt; adjust
amounts of each until the desired color is achieved. Spread out on cookie sheet.
Bake at 350 degrees for 10 minutes. Let cool, and then break up clumps with
the back of a spoon. Put all the salt into a saucer or shallow bowl.*

*Now moisten the edge of a highball glass with a wedge of lime. Roll the
outer rim of the glass through the salt. Shake off any excess into the sink.
Then you are ready to pour your favorite Bloody Mary from its shaker
into the prepared glass. Voila! Now both of you are all dressed up and
ready to party!*

—Buffy van Worthington, Park Avenue 4-H Leader

Life's victories, great and small, need to be acknowledged.
Whether you are honoring the accomplishment of a close
friend or gloating over a personal milestone, a Bloody Mary adds
a layer of panache to the occasion like nothing else can. Think
about it: toasting an achievement with an inferior cocktail would
be like christening a yacht with a bottle of Yoo-Hoo. The recipes
in this group differ from each other in terms of heat, complexity,
and alcohol content, but each earns its place at your celebration
thanks to an offbeat ingredient or fancy-schmancy pedigree. It
will be as worthy of accolades as the guest of honor. To make your
event all the merrier, be sure to follow the serving suggestions
provided.

Let Me Be the First to Welcome You to the Neighborhood (Petiot's Original Bloody Mary)

Serves 1

2 shots vodka
2 shots tomato juice
2 tsp. lemon juice
2–4 dashes salt
2 dashes black pepper
2 dashes cayenne pepper
3 dashes Worcestershire sauce
I lime wedge, to serve

Shake all the ingredients (minus the lime) with ice and strain into an Old Fashioned glass. Gently squeeze the lime wedge over the drink so you extract some of the juice but don't deform the fruit. Drop the wedge into the glass before serving. There's no better way to break the ice than with an ice-cold Bloody Mary.

Now where do you suppose a girl could find some cayenne pepper in this burg?

Since this is rumored to be the *prima facie* Bloody Mary, it's only fitting that it appears first in this book. Fernand Petiot (PEH-tee-oh), incidentally, is best known as the guy who first thought of combining tomato juice and vodka back in the 1920s. The Bloody Mary morphed into the more complex concoction you see on the left by the mid-thirties. Several men, including Petiot and comedian George Jessel, take credit for Bloody Mary's parentage, but to this day, neither has definitive proof. Here are a couple of solid facts:

* As Bloody Mary recipes go, this one's pretty much the industry standard. With it, you are unlikely to make your new neighbors think you are unsophisticated, let alone some ill-bred, hopped-up, card-carrying wingnut with way too much time on your hands.

> * If the conversation begins to lag, you can show off your book learnin' by mentioning Harry's New York Bar in Paris, where Petiot worked at the time of his supposed invention. Drop the name of Petiot's biggest competitor, George Jessel, for the honor of the Me First award. Then ask Mr. and Mrs. Newbie who *they* think invented the original Bloody Mary. If the debate becomes too heated, politely excuse yourself, collect your glassware, and go home.

Now you might be thinking, "I can't just march next door on a Sunday morning with a shaker full of hootch." Actually, you could. How do you think key parties get started? But there are no second chances at this sort of thing, so you don't want to scare the poor dears right off the bat. Here is an approach that is both refined and convivial:

1. Some lovely afternoon, knock on their door and casually mention to your soon-to-be new friends you've just whipped up a batch of Bloody Marys. Ask if they'd like to take a break from unpacking long enough to come over and join you in some light refreshments.

2. Do this in an outfit from J. Crew or The Gap so they can see how wholesome, humble, and non-threatening you are.

3. Make sure your entire house is tidy, as they will undoubtedly ask for a tour. Keep pets, nipple clamps, and witness protection documents hidden away until you know what sort of people you're dealing with. And if you're using cheap vodka in

the Bloody Marys, stash the bottle. Vodka is supposed to be odorless and flavorless, but let's not be
tasteless. No sense calling attention to your little
shortcut.

4. Pay attention to lighting, but stay away from
   candles (too reminiscent of *Rosemary's Baby*).

5. Music is always a nice touch and will help everybody relax. Here is a good playlist to start out
   with. The songs give a wink-wink to the theme
   of moving and making a go of life in a new place,
   and are not so overpowering that you can't have
   a nice conversation.

> "Do You Know the Way to San Jose," by
>   Dionne Warwick
> "Lonely," by Bat for Lashes
> "Better Things," by Massive Attack
> "Finally Moving," by Pretty Lights
> "Coming to America," by Neil Diamond
> "Warwick Avenue," by Duffy
> "Broke," by Modest Mouse
> "Unpacking the Suitcase," by Michael
>   Whalen
> "Home," by Michael Buble
> "Brand New Start," by Marti Pellow
> "New York, New York," by Frank Sinatra

6. Offer a light snack, but don't make it look like you're
   trying too hard. A selection of crudite works well,
   as does a basket of water crackers. If you consider
   yourself something of a cheese whiz, you could serve
   some asadero or cotija alongside. Use caution with

this, though. You don't want to bring your event to a sudden halt when your guests develop apoplexy from your brazen non-cheddar choices.

Good fences may make good neighbors, but good Bloody Marys make lifelong friends.

It Took Me All Friggin' Weekend, But I Finally Got the Grout Clean

Serves 1 to 2

4 oz. vodka
2–3 slices bacon
1 Tbsp. chopped red onions
1 Tbsp. lemon juice
1-inch fresh jalapeño
1/2 tsp. Dijon mustard
1/2 tsp. capers
6 oz. Spicy Hot V8
1/2 tsp. horseradish
1 pinch celery salt
1 pinch black pepper
1 tsp. Kahlua
1 tsp. Worcestershire sauce
Hot sauce, to taste
1 lemon wedge, to serve
1 celery stalk, to serve

Prepare bacon-infused vodka according to the directions on the next two pages. Put everything else (excluding the garnishes) in a food processor and blend well. Serve in a highball glass with the lemon wedge and celery. Spring cleaning just got a whole lot springier.

Who's ready for a Bloody Mary?
Raise your hand!

Y ou, my intrepid friend, deserve a pat on the back. Just think of all the goofing off you might have gotten done, but no! You took the bull by the horns and tackled the nasty grout. It's time to treat yourself to a reward.

* First things first. I'm all for elbow-length gloves at cocktail time, but usually something in satin and maribou, not yellow rubber. Take the infernal things off. Brush your hair.

* Now head down to the kitchen and get out 2 or 3 slices of bacon. Cut them into little strips of about 1/2-inch or so, then fry them in a skillet. When the bacon is fully cooked, pour all the bacon bits, grease included, into a small glass container; a glass measuring cup is perfect. Add your vodka, mix well, and put it in the freezer.

* While that's infusing, go take a bubble bath in your squeaky-clean tub. Candles, mud mask, the whole works. Silence your cell phone.

* When you get out, carefully review the list of ingredients and see if you're missing anything. If you are, do not—I repeat—*do not* skimp or substitute. Nothing is too good for you today! Pull on a Juicy Couture tracksuit and run out to the store for any necessaries.

* By the time you get back, your vodka should be ready. Take the vessel out of the freezer and skim off the glacier of fat that has congealed at the top. Toss the vodka and all the other ingredients into your food processor, and give them a whirl. If you like a Bloody Mary with lots of texture (not to mention protein), you can also puree the bacon pieces. But if you prefer your drinks a little less meaty, skim them out. Don't get rid of the bacon pieces entirely, though. You can bake them in a quiche or toss them into a pot of soup.

* Gather some supplies such as your favorite pillow, your significant other, a blanket, your cat, a hearty sandwich, and all twelve of the remote controls that operate your entertainment system, and choose a movie that lets you wallow in your accomplishment. Here are a few ideas:

Movies About Taking On a Challenge

Inherit the Wind
Erin Brockovich

The Pursuit of Happyness
African Queen
Finding Forrester
Australia
The Social Network
The Miracle Worker

Movies In Which Bad Things Happen to Losers

Fried Green Tomatoes
Dude, Where's My Car?
Carrie
Any Quentin Tarantino movie
Knocked Up
A Nightmare On Elm Street

Movies That Reward People for Not Giving Up

Eat Pray Love
Bells Are Ringing
Amistad
I Now Pronounce You Chuck and Larry
Music and Lyrics
Flashdance
127 Hours

Put a large quantity of ice in one of your good glasses—not the everyday ones—and pour yourself a big helping of Hooray-for-Me. Go back for seconds. Is that cell phone still on vibrate? Good girl.

Tonight's Our Anniversary and My Mom's Watching the Kids

Serves 1

- 1 shot chilled Jägermeister
- 2 tsp. salsa
- 1 32-oz. bottle Bloody Mary mix
- Green olives, to serve (optional)
- Cherry tomatoes, to serve (optional)

Pour ice-cold Jägermeister into a jelly jar, then add the salsa and a couple of ice cubes. Fill the jar to the top with your favorite Bloody Mary mix; stir well. For a garnish, try a skewer of olives and cherry tomatoes. Add a straw, and you're off and running!

You two run along and have your dirty little weekend. The children and I will be just fine.

Okay, darling girl, you've just gotten home from work and you don't have a minute to lose! Listen carefully: He's due home at 6:30 PM, so that means you've only got an hour to pull this off. Now take a deep breath, put down the car keys, and...go!

5:30 PM—Put the Jägermeister in the freezer along with two 6- or 8-ounce jelly jars.

5:35 PM—Pick up any Legos, burp rags, crayons, Hot Wheels cars, Barbie shoes, binkies, math homework, soccer cleats, teething rings, glitter barrettes, and/or Transformers you see lying around the immediate area.

5:50 PM—Take a quick shower. Shave both your legs (I know, you haven't had time to do that on the same day since that smug obstetrician announced, "It's a girl!"). Put on something sexy.

6:15 PM—Despair of finding something sexy and opt for something clean.

6:20 PM—Set the table...light a scented candle...put on some music. These songs ought to set the mood:

> "Love Faces," by Trey Songz
> "What's My Name," by Rihanna
> "If This World Were Mine,"
>   by Luther Vandross
> "Tonight," by Enrique Iglesias,
>   featuring Ludacris
> "You Are the Only Exception," by Paramore
> "Rhythm of Love," by Plain White T's
> "Love Letter," by R. Kelly
> "Spend My Life with You," by Eric Benet
> "We Both Deserve Each Other's Love,"
>   by L.T.D.

6:28 PM—Turn the Crock-Pot down to low. Remove the garlic bread from its foil condom. Apply lip gloss or A+D Ointment, whichever's handy.

6:29 PM—Assemble two Bloody Marys. There are only three ingredients, so you're home free. It would be even easier, of course, to simply drink shots of Jägermeister like you did on that spring break ten years ago. But you're older now—practically thirty!—with a family and responsibilities, so you need a tipple with a little more sophistication. This recipe lets you have it all— the tomato juice for your mature side, the Jägermeister for your youthful side, and the salsa to remind you that even the most responsible young adult needs to kick up her heels once in a while.

6:30 PM—Place one drink in the free hand of the grinning man bearing flowers.

6:31–9:29 PM—Dinner...dancing...none of your business...drooling on his shoulder as you slide off into an unintentional nap...

9:30 PM—Vow to do something really, *really* nice for your mother soon.

The Pregnancy Test Was Negative

Serves 1

Salt
1 jigger dry sherry
1 Tbsp. lime juice
4 oz. tomato juice
3 drops Tabasco sauce
3 drops Worcestershire sauce
1 pinch celery salt
1 pinch black pepper
1 celery or carrot stick, to serve

Lightly salt the rim of a pilsner glass and fill with ice. Pour in the sherry, lime juice, and tomato juice. Mix well, then add seasoning. Garnish with a celery or carrot stick. (And if you're literally throwing a negative-pregnancy-test party, you can up the cute factor by writing "EPT" on popsicle sticks to use as stirrers.)

All hail Queen Mary and the vestal virgins of Marin County!

There's nothing quite like a Little Bundle from Heaven. A Bun in the Oven. Our Little Miracle. The Pitter-Patter of Little Feet. Without babies, whose cheeks would we pinch? Who would we rock to sleep? Whose babbling would fill us with such delight? Besides Jon Hamm, I mean.

On the other hand, there are bona fide reasons to rejoice when the stork flies right on by.

1. After your purebred, costs-more-than-your-car, just-came-into-heat pooch gets busy at the dog park the minute your back is turned.

2. When you stop to consider the ramifications of no alcohol, no seafood, no caffeine, no hot tubs, and no being able to see your feet for several

months. Oh, and let's not forget cankles and your hormone-frenzied attempts to wrap them around your significant other, even though that's what got you into this mess to begin with.

3. When you've recently had a baby, and everyone, including Dr. Oz and your best friend and the guy who came to fix the water heater and your Aunt Mildred, knows you can't get pregnant while breastfeeding...right?

4. When your 30-something, unemployed, clinically depressed roommate "IS JUST LATE THIS MONTH BECAUSE OF STRESS! GEEZ!"

5. When you can't tell if Sarah Ferguson has peri-menopausal bloat or...not.

6. When the teenager sitting next to you on the bus teaches you Welfare Algebra: baby + baby + baby + (new boyfriend + potential baby) − boyfriend = bigger checks.

Honey, don't kid yourself. There's playing it safe and there's dodging a bullet, and savvy gals know the difference. So before you break a nail patting yourself on the back, let's take a minute to see if you can tell the difference between smart planning and dumb luck.

Playing It Safe	Dodging a Bullet
Having an unlisted phone number	Screening calls
Umbrellas	Valet parking
Maxing contributions to your 401K	Winning the Powerball
Knowing how to change a tire	AAA
Three-day juice fast	Spanx
Learning to foxtrot for your sister's wedding	She picks a salsa band
Interviewing at a new tech company	Figuring out they're telemarketers

Okay, enough with the self-analysis. It's time for a cocktail. The Pregnancy Test Was Negative Bloody Mary is loaded with class and good taste, yet it's so easy to do, you'll feel like you forgot something. The bright, not-quite-sweet flavor is a surprise if your mouth was expecting vodka, and it will show your friends that you're not afraid to take risks. On the other hand, if you happen to be the guest of honor at this particular event, that cat may already be out the bag. Your Dumb Luck genes will make sure you have enough pilsner glasses to go around. The Smart Planner side of you will already have all the fixings for this drink in your alphabetized, un-childproofed, savvy-gal pantry. Why not throw one together any time congratulations are in order, whether you earned them or not? Nobody's keeping score. Now get out of those baggy clothes and throw on a Billie Holiday CD. Call a few close friends, or not. Do a victory lap around the block. Braid Queen Anne's Lace into your hair. Knock on wood. Better yet, do all of the above. You can't be too careful...or can you?

Tell Us Again How He Proposed (Hemingway's Perfect Bloody Mary)

Serves 4 to 6

  1 ice chunk (the biggest that will fit in a large pitcher)
  1 pint vodka
  1 pint chilled tomato juice
  1 Tbsp. Worcestershire sauce
  1 jigger fresh lime juice
  Several drops Tabasco sauce
  1 pinch each of celery salt, cayenne pepper, black pepper
  Garnish assortment: 1–2 celery stalks per drink plus 1
    jar each of green olives, pickled green beans or okra,
    banana peppers, pepperoncini, asparagus, and cocktail
    onions

Pour all of the ingredients except the garnish assortment into a large pitcher and stir. Keep on stirring, and then taste it to see how it is doing. If it is too powerful, weaken it with more tomato juice. If it lacks authority, add more vodka. Pour into highball glasses, leaving room at the top for the garnish. Arrange the small garnish items on skewers; stand the larger ones upright in the glass.

I wish I'd been more clear when I said I'd always wanted a big rock.

Assuming you said yes and are now, in fact, betrothed, this is an occasion to get all your girlfriends together for a little envy-tinged squealing. Invite them over so they can hear every critical detail and sample your delicious, all-grown-up-now Bloody Marys. Why channel Hemingway, you ask? Besides knowing how to make a fine-tasting drink, he was well known for being a master of understatement and grace under pressure. You want to share your news with style, not gloat like a starry-eyed rube. Here's how to bring off your fete without putting your foot in your mouth.

1. Serve each guest her Bloody Mary in a different style of glass. Drop hints about wanting a nice matching set of barware for a wedding present.

2. Supply a lot of garnish (refer to the list at left). This is an important tip for any public speaking event. If your audience is busy chewing, they will be less

likely to interrupt you. Even better if the garnish is spicy. No one will be able to catch their breath, let alone talk.

3. While all eyes are focused on you, hold your glass in your left hand with The Ring facing the room. Be sure it has good direct lighting. If the diamond is over five carats, position your hand so you don't blind anyone. And try to hold still—the strobe effect of your fidgeting can cause seizures, especially among the elderly or insanely jealous.

Topics to cover during the first round of drinks: where you were, what you wore, what he said, and how surprised you were. Move on to Round 2 if you (sad to say): (a) were at a Justin Bieber concert, (b) were naked, (c) blackmailed him into popping the question, or (d) swallowed the ring that was cleverly hidden in your pot de crème.

Topics to cover during Round 2: your parents' reaction; expected date, location, and size of the wedding; and potential honeymoon plans. Move on to Round 3 if: (a) your parents aren't back from Burning Man yet so they don't know; (b) the wedding will hopefully be before your third trimester; (c) you'll only be able to pick one bridesmaid; (d) your groom's parole officer won't let him leave the state.

Topics to cover during Round 3: how you knew he was The One, and the fact that he has charming single friends if anyone's interested. Move on to Round 4 if anyone is crying, especially you.

Topics to cover during Round 4: anything previously avoided, because no one's going to remember anything you say from here on out.

I Landed the Account, Bitchez

Serves 1

- 1 part (approximately 2 shots) tomato-flavored vodka (Three Olives or Crop Organic are good brands)
- 1 part Scotch
- 1 part tomato juice
- 1/8 tsp. freshly ground black pepper
- 6–8 dashes Tabasco sauce
- 1 tsp. Worcestershire sauce
- 1 tsp. grated onion
- 1 rosemary sprig, to serve (optional)

Combine all the ingredients in a cocktail shaker and mix well. Strain over ice cubes in an Old Fashioned glass. This is intended to be a single serving, but everyone has their own interpretation of the word "part." If you choose to garnish, slap a sprig of rose*Mary* against your palm (aka, in the era before all the hoo-ha about sexual harassment, "spanking your Rosemary") and stick it in the drink as you would a straw. Swish it around a bit, and then take it out before sipping. You don't want it to PowerPoint you right in the eye.

I owe it all to the swell folks at Hi-Life Business College.

This is no time for false modesty. Those seventy-hour work-weeks, Sunday morning conference calls, and world-class schmoozing have finally paid off. Yessiree, you're wearing the big girl pants now! You deserve a libation that tastes like Wall Street, private jets, and Hermès suits. The taste of winning. Let the sales department swill martinis. Give the graphic designers their Syrah. The copywriters shall have IPA. But for you, hotshot, only a Bloody Mary will do. You know why? Because winners do not drink cocktails with umbrellas in them. Winners do not order things called "Sex on the Beach" or "Fuzzy Navel." Winners are not seen holding beverages that come in pastel colors. Winners, as you well know, start revolutions. Incite envy, lust, and respect. Make history. So the Bloody Mary at the end of your arm on this occasion has big shoes to fill. It's got to be sleek and cutting-edge.

Pared-down but complex. Every artfully chosen ingredient doing its job. Visually arresting. One that delivers on its promise. You know what to do.

Get the conga line to let you down off their shoulders. Make your way over to the fully stocked bar in your new corner office. Better yet, send a minion or two to do your bidding. Loosen your collar, slip off your shoes, and settle your successful butt in a comfy chair (first thing tomorrow, order that chair you've always wanted—the one made from the hides of cows that receive daily shea butter massages from Portuguese courtesans, and has seven motors to control the temperature, postural support, media feed, erogenous zone stimuli, aromatherapy, and mineral infusions). This is probably not a drink you will want two of, so make every sip an ROI. After today, it just might be your calling card. What would James Bond be without the 'shaken, not stirred' martini? Take a minute and evaluate the selling points of the drink you're about to enjoy.

* **In the Glass:** The color is similar to a rare and juicy cut of prime rib. In a certain light, it reminds you of that Ferrari Rosso Corsa coupe you've had your eye on. Powerful and inscrutable, like you, with a solid linking strategy. Hold it up to your nose. It smells like the merger of Rachel Ray and Donald Trump. The heady pheromone funk emanating from the crosshairs of Wieden + Kennedy.

* **On Your Tongue:** Take a decent-sized swig. Imagine that the Scotch is the strategist, the vodka is the client, the tomato juice is the project manager, and the spices are the creative team. Hold it in your mouth for a moment just to let them get better acquainted. This is a team-building exercise, so don't let anyone grandstand, but make a mental note about who the strongest player is. Before the

next meeting, consider allowing that one to really dominate, just to see where it takes the project, or holding it on a tighter leash. You're the boss. Or you will be by this time next year.

* **Down the Hatch:** Now swallow. You'll notice how the tomato flavor depreciates as it makes its way down the line. Vodka and Scotch employ some interstitial positioning. Onion follows the 80:20 rule—a little bit makes a big impact. Dash off a Twitter post about your findings.

Okay, enough work for one day. Whoops, you've got a little tomato juice on your shirt. Or is that lipstick? Heh. Winner take all, indeed.

My Daughter's New Boyfriend Isn't an Asswipe

Serves 1

I jigger Bakon vodka (or see instructions on page 8)
4 oz. spicy Bloody Mary mix
I Tbsp. maple syrup
1/4 tsp. chipotle Tabasco sauce
1/4 tsp. liquid smoke
Pickled okra, to serve
Cocktail onions, to serve
Blue cheese, to serve
I celery stalk, to serve

Mix the liquid ingredients in a shaker, and then strain the mixture over ice cubes in a highball glass. Garnish with pickled okra, cocktail onions, and a celery stalk filled with blue cheese. Tip: the wider the mouth of the glass, the more garnish you'll be able to use. (Finally, having a big mouth is a good thing!)

I stopped worrying about the age difference once I got a look at the size of his tool.

What was the name of her first crush? You know, that sweet boy from marching band—the oboe player. She had just gotten her braces, and she was so worried about poking him in the face with one of the wires. He gave her a red rose on her thirteenth birthday. She preserved it with hairspray, and to this day, ten years later, it's still lying on her dresser. They made each other mix tapes, studied together, took walks in the rain. She was head-over-heels crazy about him. For the next several years, though, she was just plain crazy. She managed to find boys that even their own mothers wouldn't claim. Remember some of these?

* **The soulful one** who didn't work, didn't drive, didn't bathe, didn't vote, didn't finish high school, and didn't see anything wrong with ditching her to go play in a garage band with his loser friends.

* **The covering-all-the-bases one** who was anatomically male, philosophically female, emotionally five,

intellectually forty, spiritually Wiccan, and financially parasitic.

* **The preppie one** who apparently had five or six stunt doubles to be able to cheat on her as much as he did.

* **The exotic one** from Uruguay who had trouble speaking in complete sentences, English or otherwise, unless he had a sufficient number of bong hits first. And even then, his sentence choice had to do with how his love for her precluded his need to wear a condom.

* **The romantic one** who wrote beautiful love letters over the internet, whispered sweet nothings on the phone, and fashioned jewelry for her from the change he got back at the coffee shop where they first met; but dropped her like a hot potato because he saw her TALKING TO ANOTHER BOY.

But this latest one, whom you finally met last night,

* had a polite conversation with you (you've got to be kidding!),
* helped her with her coat (gasp!),
* opened the passenger door of his new-ish Prius for her (stop it!),
* and took her to a concert (yay!),
* for which he bought tickets in advance (it's a miracle!),
* with his own money (oh, come on!),
* and which featured one of her favorite bands (wowee!),

* AND he brought her home at a decent hour (hallelujia!).

This calls for a toast. And some Swag Surfin'.

If you don't happen to have bacon-infused vodka lying around all ready to go, don't you worry. You can buy bacon-flavored vodka at the liquor store. Or if you don't plan to drink it for a few hours, you can infuse it yourself. Either way, this Bloody Mary is a great little eye-opener, since you probably stayed up all night naming the babies they're going to have. All you need is a poached egg and some toast, and you've got the equivalent of a Denny's Grand Slam breakfast. The smoky hot sauce really brings the maple-bacon duo out nicely, but where there's smoke, there isn't necessarily fire. Meaning, it's not overwhelming in the spice department. After all, considering the worry that girl's put you through, you should be a little nicer to whatever is left of your stomach lining. In a universe of spicy/savory Bloodies, the little sunbreak of sweetness in this one is a delightful surprise. Just like Boyfriend of the Month.

Now you know why people say "Cheers!"

The Bloody Paparazzi

There's a little doohickey in your brain called the reticular cortex, and its job is to control how much attention you're going to give to the billions of pieces of data coming at you every day. Did you ever buy a car and then suddenly see that exact make and model all over town? Or adopt a Boston terrier and then begin to see his breed in ads, playing on the beach, and on greeting cards? Have you ever worn a new pair of shoes to a party and then see that the hostess is wearing them too? (Actually, that's not your reticular cortex; that's just a bummer.) Congratulations, you have a healthy reticular cortex!

I predict that it won't be long before you'll start to notice Bloody Mary, both the nickname and the actual drink, popping up everywhere you look. Your reticular cortex may be partly to blame, but that phrase is gaining a foothold in popular culture on a variety of levels. Either that or Bloody Marys are increasingly on the radar of newshounds and gossipmongers worldwide. Take a look at these recent and not-so-recent sightings.

Bloody Mary was a character in James Michener's *Tales of the South Pacific*. The book was later made into a musical, then into a motion picture in 1958. Mary, played by the incomparable Juanita Hall, was a native Pacific Islander who sold shrunken heads and generally led sailors astray during World War II. She earned her nickname from the color of her teeth. According to her eponymous theme song, she was fond of chewing betel nuts, which can stain teeth and skin red, and are known for causing a sensation of heat and inebriation in the body. Ring any bells?

In September of 2000, the band Five for Fighting released an album called *America Town*, and it includes a song called "Bloody Mary." The chorus goes: "Bloody Marys for all, Bloody Marys for all." I thought it was a happy hour song until I learned it's about a prostitute. Color *my* face red.

Richie Tenenbaum of *The Royal Tenenbaums* can often be seen enjoying a Bloody Mary. Ditto Mother Jefferson in the sitcom *The Jeffersons*. Fiona of *Burn Notice* and the whole Sterling/Cooper/Draper/Price staff on *Mad Men* are regularly seen drinking them as well.

DC Comics, created by Karl and Barbara Kesel, made Bloody Mary a graphic novel heroine. She is an energy vampire who can suck the life out of her victims, which allows her to mentally control them. She also projects manipulative energy through her eyes, and she hates being touched; she will kill anyone who tries to get close to her. Come to think of it, she sounds just like my sister.

Bloody Mary appears in the video game *Twisted Metal: Black*. She is a girl who is so scarred by unrequited love that it drives her to insanity and a series of killing sprees. Onscreen, she wears the bloodied wedding gown of one of her victims. She is later sent to Blackfield Asylum where I hear it's really hard to meet guys.

Quips that make fun of decapitation, amputation, disease, and/or death are known as Bloody Marys. For instance: what do you call a kid with no arms or legs? Matt. And if he's in the bathtub? Bob.

Milan's gothic rock band, Bloody Mary, has been touring throughout England and France to promote their five albums. Pretty impressive, since they've only been a band since 2000. You may have already heard vocalist Aldebran and not realized it; he recorded a voice-over for a television ad for Moschino Friends Man perfume.

Mary, Mary, Bloody Mary is a lesbian vampire movie made in 1975. It stars Christina Ferrare and John Carradine. There's probably a very good reason why no one has heard of it before, but you can't blame them for trying.

PART II

Incantations

You can prepare me a small rhesus negative Bloody Mary.
   —Monty, *Withnail & I*

Wishing on a star, sitting on Santa's lap, blowing out birth-day candles, putting a tooth under your pillow...there are lots of rituals we were taught as children to help us get what we wanted. We're not kids anymore, but we still want things. (I know I do.) So it only makes sense to learn how to wish for them in less childish ways. These next eight Bloody Marys are already a dream come true: seductively spicy, intoxicatingly smooth. The secret to their alchemy is in the magick ingredients. Master these recipes, and you won't be needing that rabbit's foot anymore.

Maybe They Won't Notice I Burned the Steaks

Serves 1

Salt
Chili powder
3 oz. V8 juice
2 Tbsp. fresh lime juice
1/2 tsp. Worcestershire sauce
1/2 tsp. hot sauce
Beer, preferably Tecate or Dos Equis
    (nothing too sweet)

Heavily salt the rim of a 12-ounce plastic cup, using a 1:1 mixture of salt and chili powder. Combine the next four ingredients in the prepared cup, then add enough beer to fill it. Gently stir to blend, as any salt that falls into the beer will create too much foam. And that's a distraction of the wrong sort entirely.

If God had meant for me to be a good cook, he wouldn't have given me this cleavage.

The best way to tell that winter is officially over is not the appearance of Punxsutawney Phil or the first fragile crocus popping up in the backyard. It's the wagon train of shopping carts leaving Sam's Club heaped with weed 'n feed, charcoal briquettes, and cases of beer. The smell of sunblock and lawnmower exhaust in the air. The steady hum of leaf blowers, curious insects, and zippers opening to reveal the pasty flesh underneath. Berry picking! Garage sales! Frisbees! Pool parties!!!

Hold on, pump the brakes for a minute, sweetheart. You've forgotten one simple truth. Martha Stewart you're not. Your idea of a home-cooked meal is take-and-bake pizza. The tulips in the window boxes are about as real as your Mystic Tan. But if you have your heart set on hosting a barbecue, you'll have to master a minimum of three skills: (1) making friends who can be counted on to bring really yummy potluck dishes, (2) learning how to turn on your gas grill, and (3) knowing how to make a killer summer cocktail. Luckily, this sleight-of-hand Bloody Mary is as easy as blueberry pie, and it's tasty enough to save the day even if your careful preparations go awry. It's best known by its Mexican name, Michelada.

Here's how to throw the quintessential outdoor party:

1. Hire a couple of bored neighbor kids to help you spruce up the backyard. If you can't find any, there are a number of tactics you can use to camouflage the party area.

   * Schedule the event after dark.
   * Cover the mess with bed sheets; tell guests you are about to have the house painted.
   * Gaily announce that it's a *Gray Gardens* theme and give everyone a sweater to wear on his or her head. (If they don't get the reference, gather everyone around and tell them this spellbinding story. If *you* don't get the reference, get thee to Netflix immediately!)

2. Scatter chairs around in cozy groupings, but close to a fire exit—just in case.

3. Set up a table in the shade that's large enough for side dishes, condiments, napkins, paper plates, Pepto-Bismol, Neosporin, and Band-Aids.

4. Wear something that will set tongues to wagging, such as an arresting piece of jewelry, an ostentatious hat, a codpiece, or a *lucha libre* mask. Put a Tito Puente record on the hi-fi.

5. Rim several cups with the salt mixture and set aside. You could even put the V8 and seasonings into each cup ahead of time just to speed things along.

6. As your guests begin to arrive, top off each cup with ice-cold beer and stir to blend. Hand everyone a drink right off the bat so you can turn your attention to the food.

7. Lose track of what's on the grill because of all the clamoring for more Micheladas.

8. Drop the charred remains of the T-bones into a bucket of water and shoo guests toward the buffet table. No one need be the wiser.

The Way to a Man's Heart Is Through His Stomach, But That's Not Where I'm Headed

Serves 10 to 12

- 46-oz. bottle Campbell's tomato juice
- 1 garlic clove
- 1/2 avocado
- 1/4 cup Worcestershire sauce
- 2 oz. lemon juice
- 2 Tbsp. steak sauce
- 2 tsp. cracked black pepper
- 2 tsp. celery salt
- 2 tsp. hot sauce
- 1 tsp. horseradish
- 1 fifth of inexpensive vodka
- 10–12 pickled asparagus spears, to serve
- 10–12 celery stalks, to serve

Excluding the vodka and garnishes, whir the rest of the ingredients together in a blender or food processor. Fill pint glasses with ice and 2 shots of vodka each. Top with the tomato mixture, then garnish with an asparagus spear and a stalk of celery. Serve with a paper napkin that has your phone number (or room number) clearly written on it.

(Psstt...this recipe was voted "most liked" in Portland's 2012 Distiller's Bloody Mary Taste-off!)

*Why don't you lose that uniform
and show me why they call you boys
"mounties?"*

W arning to the faint of heart: you're about to meet Bloody
Mary's seedier cousin. And I'm not talking about lemons
here, people. This is the Bloody Mary that will get his attention. Or get you that second date. Or just get your ladybits the
adoration they've been craving. Sure, it's got a lot of vodka in
it, but the real value add is that it's a steaming smorgasbord of
carnal pleasures. You've got the basics on the list: tomato juice,
Worcestershire sauce, lemon, pepper, and celery salt. That's your
grandmother's Bloody Mary. We're going to take that, put some
gold lamé stilettos on it, and teach it to twirl around a pole. Let
me show you what I mean.

Garlic: Greeks and Egyptians discovered garlic's aphrodisiac
properties thousands of years ago. Modern research has proven
that eating garlic improves the circulation, which enhances both
sexual enjoyment and performance. Tibetan monks were forbid-
den to enter the temple if they had been eating garlic because
it made them more likely to think about monkey business than
monk business. No wonder it's classified as a "hot" herb.

Avocado: The many nutrients in an avocado contribute to luscious skin and a vigorous, healthy heart. They were once prized by the Aztecs for curing erectile dysfunction. (The Aztecs called them *ahucatl*, which translates to "testicle.") For many ancient tribes, avocados were not only useful as a sexual stimulant in this life but the next: avocado seeds from the eighth century BC were found buried with a Peruvian mummy—just in case he still had plans to hook up, I suppose.

Chili peppers: These phallic little beauties are known to stimulate endorphins, which are chemicals released by the brain that give you a natural rush, like the feeling you get when you're really crushing on someone. In sufficient quantities, they also raise your pulse rate and make you sweat. Any liquid hot sauce containing capsaicin, the essence that makes spicy food spicy, will do the trick. Then again, so will Tom Jones.

Steak sauce: While not scientifically proven, there is something about the flavor of meat that pings on the average man's caveman DNA. He'll have a sudden urge to carry you off by the hair and drag his knuckles all over you.

Horseradish: In medieval times, horseradish pulp was widely used as a marital aid. The US Food and Drug Administration says there's no such thing as an aphrodisiac. Don't date anyone who works there.

Asparagus: Well, come on…just look at it. But it's more than a suggestive accessory. Asparagus has the added benefit of being a good source of vitamin E, which contributes to the production of sex hormones.

Celery: This underrated vegetable just so happens to stimulate the pituitary gland, a key player in the sex hormone starting lineup.

Besides that, after it's eaten, a pheromone called androstenone is excreted through the skin and has a libidinous effect on women. Pssht. Like you needed another excuse to sit on his lap.

Oh yes, you'll need a little atmosphere to go along with your ulterior motives. For best results, try to hit all five of his senses like they've never been hit before. You've already nailed taste. Here are some ideas for the other four.

* **Smell:** A dab of perfume on your pulse points (neck, wrists, backs of knees) is a given. Not too much. Also, put something heavenly in the oven like a loaf of bread or a roast. On both counts, though, once he smells it, he's not going to rest until he gets some, so be prepared to deliver the goods.

* **Sound:** Don't waste time with subtlety. Put these on your boom box:

    > "Pour Some Sugar On Me," by anybody
    >   (there are LOTS of covers of this song)
    > "You Can Leave Your Hat On," by Joe
    >   Cocker
    > "Put Your Hands On Me, Baby," by Joss
    >   Stone
    > "I Want Your Sex," by George Michael
    > "Let's Get It On," by Marvin Gaye
    > "Battleflag," by Lo Fidelity All-Stars
    > "Fever," by Peggy Lee
    > "So Good," by Pharoahe Monch
    > "Dirty Desire," by Utada
    > "Put It In," by Storm Large
    > "Love to Love You, Baby," by Donna
    >   Summer

"In My Bed," by Amy Winehouse
"Swing," by Savage
"Glory Box," by Portishead
"I'm Gonna Love You Just a Little More,
    Baby," by Barry White

* **Sight:** Candlelight is the most flattering and provocative, provided your tryst is planned for the evening hours. Wardrobe-wise, steer toward shades of red, but if you know red doesn't look especially good on you, try accenting with red shoes, toenail polish, watchband, or something similar. Another way to go is to plant touches of red around The Room, such as a pillow or a lampshade. Even better, bring home a dozen red roses and write "Can't wait to see you again" on the card. He'll be half-mad with jealousy and putty in your hands.

* **Touch:** No hairspray. No wool. No stubble. No excuses.

Now you're probably wondering: if this is such a sure-fire man-getter of a recipe, why did you have to make such a big batch? Duh. 'Cause all your friends are going to want some too.

Remind Me Why I'm Going Skydiving Tomorrow

Serves 1

 1 oz. vodka
 Splash of olive brine
 1/2 tsp. barbecue sauce
 Dash cayenne pepper

Fit all of the above ingredients into a 1½- or 2-ounce shot glass, stir with a toothpick, and have at it. (It's also good with a beer chaser.) Repeat as needed.

I'm so nervous, I don't know if I'm coming or going!

If you ask me, staring fear in the face is not exactly a character-builder; it's actually quite the opposite. I just want to hunker down into my Pampers and suck my thumb. What I wouldn't give for a little shot o' courage! I'd toss it down with aplomb, like Humphrey Bogart, throw out my chin, and tackle fear head-on. Generally speaking, that's a much better look for most people than hunkering and thumb-sucking, wouldn't you say?

Oh, I'm not fooling anyone, least of all myself. I'm scared of almost everything. Spiders, global warming, calcium deficiency, fascist regimes, failure, heights, running out of Urban Decay lip gloss...well, you get the idea. When I find myself shaking in my proverbial boots, I square my shoulders, look myself right in the eye, take a deep breath, and repeat the words my dad always said to me: "Winners never quit, and quitters never win!" He found many occasions to impart this particular advice, including:

* when I accidentally signed up for dodgeball on Electives Day in fourth grade

* when I gave the school bully all my lunch money so he'd stop punching me

* during my sixteenth hour of labor

* after I walked to the end of the high dive and practically fainted on the spot

* when I broke my Hollywood Juice Fast diet with a giant stack of pancakes

Besides being taught how to persevere and to keep myself mired in situations I had no business being in, I've learned over the years that there are hundreds of different phobias out there, and millions of people suffering from them *as we speak*. This little powerhouse of a Bloody Mary is guaranteed to take the edge off whatever your particular bogeyman is. It's got everything you need, and no weird, anxiety-producing ingredients. The sweetness of the barbecue sauce is perfectly offset by the olive brine, similar to how machismo is best balanced by reason. The vodka will steady your nerve endings just before the cayenne comes along and singes them off. *Voila!* No more fear. And you'll look cool drinking it, devoid as it is of umbrellas, straws, or other frou-frou. Just hold it up at eye level, say my dad's immortal phrase, and gulp it down. For even more street cred, you could add, "Here's blood in your eye." The beer chaser you can nurse as long as you like.

A note of caution before you throw all of it to the wind. Those individuals that experience the following fears should not indulge in this drink:

Aerophobia	Fear of swallowing air
Anablephobia	Fear of looking up
Aritmophobia	Fear of numbers, calculations
Dipsophobia	Fear of drinking
Ereuthophobia	Fear of the color red
Geumaphobia	Fear of taste
Hedonophobia	Fear of pleasure
Hyalophobia	Fear of glass
Kainophobia	Fear of anything new
Methyphobia	Fear of alcohol
Microphobia	Fear of small things
Thermophobia	Fear of heat

Who's still with me??? Bully for you! Spoken like a true winner. Let's forget about skydiving and have another Bloody Mary.

When I Win the Lottery, I'm Quitting This Crappy Job

Serves 1

   Several corn chips, crushed
   1 jigger Jose Cuervo Gold tequila
   4 oz. tomato juice
   1/2 tsp. finely grated horseradish
   1/2 tsp. Worcestershire sauce
   1/2 tsp. chopped serrano pepper
   1 pinch each of kosher salt, pepper, celery seeds
   1 tsp. smoky- or hickory-flavored barbecue sauce
   1 dash fresh lemon juice, or to taste
   Tabasco sauce, to taste
   Cucumber slices and olives, to serve

Coat the rim of an Old Fashioned glass with crushed corn chips. Shake the next nine ingredients with ice and strain into the prepared glass. Garnish with cucumber and plenty of olives. Serve with a scowl.

If and when I want my ass pinched, I'll go to Rome, thank you very much!

Aww, hard day at the office? Take off your coat and pull up a chair. I've made a movie for you. That's right! It's called *Warts in the Alley**, and it's the story of a brave girl who decides not to take any more guff. Oh wait, let me make you a Bloody Mary first. You'll see why in a minute. (* = diner-speak for a side order of olives)

Exterior, day: A sun-baked street in downtown Shady Pines, Arkansas. A woman strides into view—no, that's not exactly right—the back of a woman stomps into view, muttering her way to the bus station. She's wearing beat-to-hell white leather oxfords and a polyester waitress uniform the color of French's mustard. One hand is carrying the tip jar she stole from the diner; the other is busy yanking the stupid little white cap out of her hair. She's intent on putting some miles between her and that shitty boss of her—well, former boss now. That lucky right cross that busted his nose earned her the nickname "Bloody Mary" and a one-way trip to the unemployment line.

Mary: Well, he had it comin'. Tryin' to feel me up like a big hothouse tomayta. I showed him that ain't no way to treat a lady.

This Bloody Mary has so much character, I just had to introduce her to you as, well, a character. She's gutsy and strong with a heart of gold—Cuervo Gold, to be exact. She comes from humble, time-honored roots like Worcestershire sauce and horseradish, but the barbecue sauce takes out the frump factor. True, she's on the small side, but there's no doubt she's a handful. She doesn't make any apologies or take any lip. One warning: be sure to follow the recipe exactly. Don't try to use more tequila or chopped pepper (or whatever) than it calls for. If you get overeager with any part of her, you'll knock the whole thing out of kilter and she'll make you pay. Either your head will be on fire tomorrow or your nether parts will. Her boss learned that the hard way.

Interior, day: Middle-aged man in greasy cook's apron lies sprawled on the green and white checkerboard floor. He sits up partway and notices his nose is bleeding. After he struggles to his feet, he looks at his reflection in the blade of a cleaver and groans.

Boss (admiringly): That little gal sure doesn't pull any punches, she *gives* 'em. I hope the next guy she tangles with treats her with respect.

When you behave yourself, Mary doesn't wear out her welcome. Wham, bam, thank you, ma'am. Before you know it, all you'll see is the bus doors closing and that squashed white cap blowing down the street. Take a tip from spunky gals everywhere: when you've had enough, don't take any more guff. Go back to the office tomorrow with your head held high and an ultimatum, not to mention a stray celery seed or two, on your lips.

I Know We Just Met, But I Want to Have Your Babies

Serves 1

Celery salt
1 jigger Baileys Irish Cream
1 32-oz. bottle Bloody Mary mix
3–4 dashes Tabasco sauce
1 pickle spear, to serve
Filberts, to serve

Rim a coffee mug with celery salt (moisten first by rubbing the edge of the glass with one of the pickles), fill it 3/4 full with ice cubes, and then pour the Baileys into it. Fill the remaining 1/4 with the Bloody Mary mix, and stir gently to combine. Before serving, garnish with the pickle spear and filberts (for maximum effect, you'll also need two straws and a pair of handcuffs).

Wanna play house?
I'll be the mommy.

Hmmm? No, I didn't hear anything. Ticking? Oh, that. That's just my biological clock. Pay no attention. Here, I'll turn up Celine Dion so it won't bother you. It's just that it's ticking so insistently these days, I hardly know what to do anymore...well, except...no, I couldn't possibly ask...oh, here goes. If we were to, you know, get married and start a family, I'd...no, wait! We're still five blocks from my house! Where are you going?? Oh...hey, call me!

Extreme, right? You'd never stoop so low, right? Well, how do you intend to snag the big lug if you're going to go about it all subtle-like? Here, wipe that dejected pout off your face and get ready to take some notes.

The first thing you need to understand is that he probably has no idea how you feel. That's because men and women, through some DNA-related design flaw, speak entirely different languages. Before you have another heartfelt conversation with your beau, use this handy glossary to make sure you're getting your point across in a way he can understand.

Keyword	Women's Definition	Men's Definition
Vulnerable (*vul-ne-ra-bul*)	Fully opening one's self emotionally to another person	Playing football without a cup
Communication (*ko-myoo-ni-kay-shun*)	The open sharing of thoughts and feelings	Leaving a note before taking off on a fishing trip
Commitment (*ko-mit-ment*)	The desire to fully bond with another person and start a family	Trying not to hit on other women while on a date with you
Making Love (*may-king luv*)	The greatest expression of intimacy a couple can achieve	Call it whatever you want as long as we get to do it

Next, pay close attention to atmosphere. He already knows you're witty, sexy, fun, successful, charming, adventurous, sentimental, independent, and loving. And while those things are still very important, he also needs to see your mature, responsible-yet-easygoing, maternal side. That doesn't mean Play-Doh under your fingernails, but it does hint at being fairly low-maintenance. If you're predisposed to such things, forego the helmet hair, the false eyelashes, and the dry-clean-only Trina Turk blouse. If his glass leaves a ring on the coffee table, don't freak out. If you own a dog (and for your sake I hope it's not the kind you carry in your purse and dress in diamanté), you don't have to go as far as letting it sleep on your bed, but be sure your guy sees you romping around with it. Cats, gerbils, and boa constrictors just send the wrong message; lock them in the back bedroom for the time being. Bonus points: (1) arrange to have snapshots of other people's children all over your refrigerator, (2) put Mr. Yuk stickers on your cleaning supplies, (3) cut the crusts off his sandwiches.

You're almost there. All you've got to do now is put Mommy where your—er, his—mouth is. This creamy, dreamy Bloody Mary is the icing on the oatmeal cookies. It goes together in seconds and requires no futzing with gadgets or complicated preparations. You'll want to serve it in a mug for two reasons: one, it's an offbeat and some say unpalatable color, and the mixture can curdle on you; mugs hide a multitude of visual sins. And two, you can give him an unabashedly cute mug, like the one you made at Outdoor School in the sixth grade. Such a mug will incite a nostalgic, tender chat (see glossary above). The best part, though, is the flavor. The first sip will remind you of an orange Creamsicle, but a second later, the spicy-salty undertones come through. It's comfort food with a kick. One minute he'll be reminiscing about skinned knees and childhood summers, and the next he'll have an uncontrollable desire to bounce babies on those knees. Before you know it, he'll be on them, begging to spend the rest of his life with you; or at the very least, begging for another of your fantastic Bloody Marys.

Here's a warning: you had better know what you're doing before subjecting the poor fellow to witchcraft like this. Results can be sudden and long-lasting.

I Want This Promotion So Bad I Can Taste It

Serves 1

> 2 shots gin
> Dash lemon juice
> 4–6 dashes Worcestershire sauce
> 6 dashes Tabasco sauce
> Black pepper, salt, and celery salt, to taste
> 4 oz. Clamato
> 1/2 tsp. horseradish
> Stuffed olives, to serve (optional)
> 1 celery stalk, to serve (optional)

Put everything but the garnishes in a cocktail shaker, shake well, and strain into a Collins glass over ice cubes. Keep the garnish streamlined and not too intense, like Hilary Clinton's pantsuits. A couple of citrus-stuffed olives and a celery stalk are good choices.

Does this outfit make my ambition look big?

From the moment this Bloody Mary lands in front of you, it's easy to see she's no pushover. She's like the girl in your building that everyone loves to hate. You know the one. She wears way too much makeup, even when walking her purebred Alfenpinscher at seven in the morning. She's a devotee of post-minimalist art, Ann Curry, and the grapefruit and egg white diet. Her porcelain veneers are perfect, but they can't quite contain the annoyance that's always trying to leak out of her brittle smile. She doesn't care one whit who you are, but she's just one meticulously frosted hair from getting all up in your business. Even the swarthy hunk that services her BMW 2002 (and her, if the rumors are true) is kept at arm's length. Is she the girl who has everything? Maybe. But that's never stopped her from wanting more.

Now, none of this is meant to imply that this Bloody Mary is off-putting in any way. On the contrary; it's meant to imply that the combination of flavors makes it gutsy, bright, and direct. Kind of like you, you corporate-ladder-climber, you.

Let's look more closely at the recipe to see what gives it such pizzazz.

Gin: It lends a sharp edge to a drink that vodka can't match. And talk about complex! Besides juniper berries, gin is also made with botanicals such as anise, cinnamon, orange peel, cucumber, rose petals, and coriander. In fact, every gin manufacturer has a secret mix of up to fifteen herbs and spices. If you need a bit of help asking for your promotion, the term "Dutch courage" came from early uses of gin by British troops in the sixteenth century. Later, it was marketed as a diuretic, so if you're worried that bloating has been holding you back professionally, it's a wise choice indeed.

Lemon juice, Worcestershire sauce, Tabasco sauce, seasonings: You're a busy woman; you've got a glass ceiling to shatter. You can't be bothered measuring things out by the quarter teaspoon. Just unscrew the cap, a few flicks of the wrist, and you're done. So sayeth His Exalted Inspirational Majesty Tony Robbins: "The key to success is to move from an activity orientation to a results orientation." Dash your way to results.

Clamato: Time is money (see above). If a drink takes longer than five minutes to consume, it's considered a spa treatment, not a cocktail. Sound asset management keeps a person, and a company, trim and fit for duty. The only person who needs more tomato-based juice than this has just been sprayed by a skunk.

Horseradish: Okay, measuring helps here, so don't scrimp. A little zing can wake up your brain, but a too-generous dollop of this stuff can be disastrous. It detracts from your credibility if your nose is running and your cheeks are striped with mascara tears.

It's just like you to toast your upcoming success with a spare but top-drawer Bloody Mary. You both possess a winning combination of traits that make you shine. Little Miss Upstart in apartment 5E should take lessons from you. Now go out there and knock 'em dead!

I Really Hope I Fit In at This New Country Club

Serves 1 to 8 (depending on how nervous you are)

Festive ice ring:
   3–4 cups distilled water (about 1 quart)
   1–2 dozen cherry tomatoes (small)
   1–2 dozen mint sprigs

Punch:
   46-oz. bottle tomato juice, chilled
   1 ½ cups vodka
   2 Tbsp. horseradish
   2 Tbsp. lemon juice
   2 Tbsp. garlic pepper Tabasco sauce
   1 liter seltzer, chilled

To make the ice ring, half-fill a 6-cup ring mold with the distilled water, and freeze approximately 2 hours. Arrange the cherry tomatoes and mint sprigs in small clusters on the ice in the ring mold, then carefully add enough water to fill. Freeze until firm.

Now for the punch. Combine tomato juice, vodka, horseradish, lemon juice, and Tabasco sauce in a large punchbowl. Just before serving, add the seltzer and the ice ring. Ladle each serving into demure little crystal cups. (If the twerps at Revolving Door Alternative School could see you now!)

Let's sing another round of "Oklahoma," then have another round of Bloody Marys!

As my mother always said, if you can't dazzle them with brilliance, baffle them with bling. Even if you're such a rube that you can't find *Madagascar* on Netflix let alone a map, you're sure to be a hit with this beautiful Bloody Mary punch. It's so classically hip, so conventionally contemporary, even the staunchest auxiliary dowager will want to know your name. Beneath the surface, it's the same old tried-and-true recipe from days gone by. What turns it from "good" to "o god" is the party finery you've dressed it in. The seltzer sparkles in your mouth like a diamond tennis bracelet. And the cherry tomato and mint tiara resting on top is the perfect accoutrement. Concerned about the red-and-green color scheme connotation? Poo. This Bloody Mary works well at any time of the year, and at any time of day for that matter. Light yet palliative, it's a lovely aperitif whether it is served at brunch or before dinner.

But if you truly have your heart set on dazzling this crowd, you'll have to have a few other tricks up your sleeve.

1. **Wardrobe:** It's a fact that people treat you better if you dress better. That doesn't have to mean expensive. Just make sure your clothes are clean and pressed, sweaters are de-pilled, shoes are polished, buttonholes equal the number of buttons, and all the zippers work. Steer clear of polyester, loud colors, ill-fitting undergarments, and fads that are enjoying their second round of popularity (if you were old enough to wear it the first time, you're much too old to get away with it now).

2. **Talking points:** Sooner or later, you're going to have to speak to somebody, or somebody will approach you. One way to prepare for this inevitability is to brush up on current events. If you're not a quick study, try this instead: people love to talk about themselves, especially in this income bracket. Come up with several questions you could ask that don't make you sound like a stalker. Remember to make eye contact, and listen carefully to their answers. Here are some examples to get you started. Generally, stay away from politics, religion, bad odors, the economy, death, racism, and negativity. In short, don't be freaky.

   Of course, the other way to look at conversation is being on the receiving end. When a person comes up to you and asks you something from the "Good Conversation Starters" column, look him or her in the eye, smile engagingly, and lie your ass off. Say something vague about whatever it is, then do one of two things: pretend to have a coughing fit, wave your hands apologetically,

Good Conversation Starters	Bad Conversation Starters
What line of work are you in?	Does your chewing gum lose its flavor on the bedpost overnight?
Where did you go on your last vacation?	What's your favorite Cyndi Lauper song?
Do you have children?	What's the sickest you've ever been?
Do you enjoy (golf, dancing, opera, train travel, Bloody Marys, etc.)?	What's the best bargain you ever got at a garage sale?
Did you grow up in this part of the country?	Does this look infected to you?
How did you and your spouse meet?	Didn't I see you at Lisa's naked lawn-bowling party?
Have you tried the (something on the buffet table)?	Is that a wig?
What do you think about (a current bestseller, celebrity gossip, the weather)?	Do you have any rolling papers on you?

and leave the room; or come back quickly with a question of your own. If, on the other hand, you are asked something from the "Bad Conversation Starters" column, all you need to do is give them a withering smile, excuse yourself, and walk away. They clearly aren't from the right side of the tracks.

3. **Music:** if you are the hostess, you will have something to say about the music selection. Don't panic. Just like your clothing, you can't go wrong with simple, classic, and low-key. Try these for starters:

> "For All We Know,"
>   by Joe Sample and Lalah Hathaway
> "Deep Powder," by The Rippingtons
> "Missing in Venice," by Rick Braun
> "Caravan of Dreams," by Peter White
> "Soulful Strut," by Grover Washington, Jr.
> "The Sweetest Taboo," by Sade
> "Back Into My Heart," by Chris Botti
> "Because of You," by Eric Darius
> "Badabing," by Dave Koz
> "Giving You the Best That I Got,"
>   by Anita Baker

The hard part is all done. Now comes the fun. Suss out the best salon in town. Get a fresh blowout and a mani-pedi. While you're there, glance over a few magazines to familiarize yourself with the headlines. Notice what the other women are wearing, good or bad. And for the love of heaven, talk to people! Any people. All people. Because after your new crowd gets a load of your Bloody Mary punch, they'll sure be talking about you.

Go Packers

Serves 1

Generous amount of Worcestershire sauce
   (preferably Lea & Perrins), 4–5 dashes
3 drops Tabasco sauce, or more to taste
3 dashes celery salt
Juice from 1 lemon wedge
2 fingers vodka
2–3 fingers tomato juice
Dill pickle spear, to serve (optional)
Garlic-stuffed green olives, to serve (optional)
Pepperoncini, to serve (optional)

Add ice to a 12-ounce plastic cup and set aside. Put the first four ingredients in a second plastic cup and add the vodka and tomato juice in the stated proportions (you should now have 4–5 fingers' worth of liquid). Pour the mixture into the first cup (the one with the ice), then pour everything back into the second cup. Keep pouring back and forth until the mixture is well blended. Carefully pour the contents back into one of the cups. Squeeze in a little more lemon juice and garnish with any of the optional items above. (Add all three if you want a meal!)

Frank? Did you remember the pickles?

*D*ear Green Bay Fans,
    I'm well aware that this is the Packers' Official Bloody Mary
Tailgate Recipe. But I'm going to let fans of the other teams know about
it too. I appreciate you being sportsmanlike and sharing your secret
recipe with the whole football-lovin' world. After all, not everyone is
lucky enough to be able to visit Lambeau Field and enjoy your special
commemorative Bloody Marys. Go Packers!
                                        Yours truly,
                                        Judy Bennett

Dear Football-Lovin' World,
    Just so you know, this is the Bloody Mary that I was told was the
official tailgate recipe of the Green Bay Packers. Whatever. Good lord,
it's not even green! Anyway, they're kind of sensitive about it, so if you

make this drink anywhere other than Wisconsin, be sure to say that it is attributed to the Packers.

Yours truly,
Judy Bennett

I love going to tailgate parties because it's the only time I get to eat like a dude. I don't think about carbs, sodium levels, tooth decay, BMI, HDL/LDL, organic fertilizer, lactose intolerance, mercury content, or even napkins. Dudes pick up food that tastes good, and put it in their mouths. Sometimes they'll even chew a couple of times before swallowing. Dudes don't mince, saute, julienne, or braise. Not in front of other dudes, anyway. If it comes out of a cooler or off a grill, it's considered food. That's why this Bloody Mary is a winner. Nothing to chop, measure, blanch, grate, or stir. Oh, there's some squeezing to be done, but no dude worthy of the name will turn down a chance to squeeze things.

You may have noticed that the recipe says to add vodka and tomato juice, but it doesn't say exactly how much. That's because it's COLD in Wisconsin, especially as it gets later in football season. Keeping the amount somewhat flexible means that you can use whatever amount of vodka in your Bloody that will keep your innards from freezing, and then fill the cup the rest of the way with tomato juice. Or maybe you're supposed to add vodka in proportion to how dejected you are that Green Bay didn't sign Brett Favre and Michael Vick. And, since dudes don't measure, we don't know for sure how much that is. I, for one, am not going to presume to tell you how much that is. I usually look for the dude with the biggest hands (he'll pour a more generous drink and keep you warm in all kinds of other fun ways). But if you don't get it right the first time, go ahead and make another. Plenty of time before the coin toss.

Oh yes. And go Packers!

I Know What You Drank Last Summer

Let's take a break from drinking for a few moments and go to the bathroom. No, silly, pull your pants back up. Stand here in front of the mirror while I tell you a story. It's a scary ghost story / urban legend that's been around for dozens of years. You can decide for yourself whether it's true or not.

It is said at slumber parties the world over that if you say "Bloody Mary" three times in front of a mirror, the ghost of a woman will appear. The legend goes like this: she was either a widow who killed her children, or a young mother whose baby was stolen from her. Either way, her grief drove her to madness and she committed suicide. Why she decided to spend eternity in a mirror instead of Bloomingdale's or The International House of Cheesecake is beyond me. But she was crazy, after all.

Now, if this story is only partly familiar to you, there are several variations depending on where you grew up. Some people chant "Mary Worth" three times instead of "Bloody Mary." Others say, "Bloody Mary, I killed your baby," or "I believe in Mary Worth." Still others, evidently with more time on their hands, say either Mary Worth or Bloody Mary one hundred times. You can make the ritual more dramatic by spinning around first, performing it at the stroke of midnight, or leaving all the lights off. Honestly, there are more methods of this game than Angelina Jolie has kids. And more theories about who Mary was too. Some say she was a witch; others claim she was a poor little nobody who was killed in a car accident. I do know that it couldn't be sweet old Mary Worth from the comics. Unless she smothered her children with advice.

So what do you get for all your trouble? Well, the visage of the dead woman will appear in the mirror, at which point she will either (a) tear your face off, (b) drive YOU insane, or (c) drag you into the mirror with her.

Now you have three more Bloody-Mary-related reasons for not showing up for work.

PART III

Conflagrations

How to Get Bloodstains Out of Fabric

1. While the blood is still wet, soak the stained area in cold water or milk overnight, or at least a few hours.

2. Mix a teaspoon of laundry detergent with a teaspoon of hydrogen peroxide. Using a clean sponge dipped in the mixture, dab at the stain until it's gone. Then wash in cold water according to the instructions on the label.

3. Before drying the article, check to see if the bloodstain is gone. If not, repeat steps 1 and 2. If still unsuccessful, remove stain with scissors, call your lawyer, or both.

He Called Out My Sister's Name In Bed

Serves 1

Dash Worcestershire sauce
Dash habanero sauce
1 jigger New Deal Distillery Hot Monkey vodka
32-oz. bottle Tabasco Extra Spicy Bloody Mary Mix
1/4 lemon
1/4 lime
3 green jalapeño-stuffed olives, to serve

Salt the rim of a pint glass and fill it with ice cubes. Put the first three ingredients in the glass and fill the remainder with the Bloody Mary mix. Crush the lemon and the lime in your fist until the juices run freely into the drink and deep-six the rinds; mix well. Garnish with the olives that you've impaled on a skewer.

It's important to throw the murder weapon a long, long way.

*H*ell *bath no fury* is right! You need an explanation. You need revenge. You need a two-dozen-roses/Carribean-cruise/diamond earrings-sized apology.

You need a drink. And a plan.

The drink: There's a very good reason why you'd want to subject yourself to blisters on your tongue and a possible ulcer. You ever wonder why people who live in hot climates eat spicy food? It's because the increase in body temperature makes you feel cooler. Besides that, it acts as a stimulant for all your senses, making you wide awake and on top of your game. Never mind that it makes you sweat, reddens your cheeks, brings tears to your eyes, and turns your bowels to water; ever since your guy's little Freudian slip, all that has already happened to you. Consider using a shatterproof glass, in case you get an overwhelming urge to chuck it at the bastard.

The plan: When he comes through the door, put the moves on him. Make sure you still have plenty of capsaicin residue on your hands. If you don't, or if you can't stomach the idea of fondling his wedding tackle just now, think of something to say the next time Weekly Sex Night rolls around. My personal favorites:

10. *Wake me up when you're done.*
9. *You won't be needing that condom. I'm pregnant anyway.*
8. *This room could use some new drapes.*
7. *My ex used to do that too, only longer.*
6. *Sorry, I had Indian food for lunch.*
5. *It's okay; I understand that sometimes happens to men your age.*
4. *Move, I can't see Jay Leno.*
3. *On second thought, I'm kinda tired.*
2. *I can't find your penis with your belly in the way.*

The best comment ever...
1. *My sister called today asking for you. How do you spell "chlamydia"?*

Of course, the other way to go, assuming that he is oblivious to the whole incident, is to pretend civility. Prepare him a nice breakfast complete with the Bloody Mary featured here. What he doesn't know is that the drink you're about to hand him may well render him impotent as well as radioactive. Biologists call this strategy aggressive mimicry. It's a form of exploitation where a predator camouflages itself as something harmless. The hapless prey is drawn into the trap while the predator simply sits and waits. You may have seen a Venus Flytrap or Debra LaFave do this. The best part? Let's see what kind of Casanova he is with that charred strip of jerky he used to call his tongue.One final note: Be sure to serve this drink with plenty of ice. Revenge really is a dish best served cold.

They Told Me It Was a Costume Party

Serves 4 to 6

32 oz. V8
2 Tbsp. soy sauce
1/4 cup Worcestershire sauce
1/2 tsp. horseradish
1/2 tsp. kosher salt
1/2 tsp. black pepper
1/4 tsp. each of cumin, garlic powder,
    celery salt, and cayenne pepper
1/2 tsp. red pepper flakes
1/4 cup Dr. Pepper
Tabasco sauce, to taste
6–9 oz. vodka
1 lemon, to serve
1 lime, to serve
4–6 pickled okra pods, to serve

Combine the first ten ingredients in a glass pitcher. Get some highball glasses and fill each with a jigger of vodka and some ice, then add the Bloody Mary mixture. Cut the lemon and lime into wedges, and garnish the glasses with one of each as well as the pickled okra. Don't get mad, and don't get even. Get Bloody.

Yes, as a matter of fact, I do feel as stupid as you look.

Things start getting pretty scary near the end of October. The shivers running up and down your spine are not your imagination. You lie awake at night, planning your next move. You slink around during the day, eavesdropping, watching, wanting information, but you don't know whom to trust. No, I'm not talking about a zombie invasion or a family of vampires moving in next door. I'm talking, you gullible goddess, about whether or not you should wear a Halloween costume to work.

If you were at the same place of employment last year as you are now, all you have to do is remember (a) what the policy was; (b) if it was followed, encouraged, or merely tolerated; and (c) if the said policy has changed since then. If the workplace is new to you, however, you're a sitting duck. Don't bother asking your new cube-mates about the usual level of corporate holiday ballyhoo; hazing in the workplace is far from dead. I don't care what the orientation manual says. I advise you, regardless of your status within the company, to carefully consider this cautionary tale. Last Halloween, Jane from accounting was determined to show

her team spirit by participating in the company-sponsored costume contest. She somehow managed to squeeze her size ten bum
into a beige size five catsuit, then hot-glued purple balloons all
over her body. She was supposed to be a bunch of grapes. Good
old Jane. What a trooper! However, three unfortunate problems
emerged.

* She couldn't sit down all day, even to use the ladies' room.

* When the occasional balloon happened to pop, the
  deflated purple rubber revealed more and more
  of the flesh-colored sausage casing beneath. Each
  poor little blob hung there like a wrinkled bruise.
  By the end of the day, she looked like she had
  narrowly escaped from the mosh pit of a Teddy
  Pendergrass concert.

* No one else was in costume. No one at all.

Needless to say, Jane has made a vow to never, under any circumstances, wear a costume in a public place. She managed to
make it through the entire day, bless her heart, with a pleasant
smile affixed to her face, even while her cheeks surely burned
with fantasies of retribution. Frankly, I'm surprised she didn't
either spit in the water cooler, key the boss's car, or both. A dulcet
veneer can only withstand so much humiliation, after all. But
enough about Jane. Let's talk about this Bloody Mary in sheep's
clothing. You're probably surprised to find Dr. Pepper on the list
of ingredients, hidden among all the usual fare. It lends a degree
of sweetness that is rare, even a tad disconcerting, in a Bloody
Mary. The carbonation also keeps things from feeling too serious
(even more so if you can give it a quick stir right before serving).
Hold that sip in your mouth for a couple of seconds. You're about

to see why you should never judge a book by its cover. Hot on the heels of that sweet first impression lurks an incendiary surprise. The cayenne, red pepper, Tabasco sauce, and horseradish rise up and sucker-punch you right in the tonsils. Savory Worcestershire and soy sauces linger last, and help to keep all the extremes in balance.The next time you develop a sudden thirst for comeuppance and tomato juice, take my advice: the safest, most dignified way to recover from a public faux pas is to stage a little private acrimony. Mix up a pitcher of Bloodies, and invite your most supportive pals over for brunch. Watch *I Love Lucy* reruns (Lucy Ricardo is the poster child for getting into and out of all manner of degradation), or listen to Milli Vanilli, Kanye West, Britney Spears, or other such "artists" who have had their fifteen minutes of shame. Hand out prizes for the best "My Most Embarrassing Moment" stories or the most colorful counterinsurgency plots. You might even tell one of your friends it's a costume party...

If You Think I'm Paying for This Haircut, You're Sadly Mistaken

Serves 1

- 2 tsp. each of kosher salt, cayenne pepper, and black pepper
- Splash of pineapple juice
- I jigger Below Deck ginger rum
- 4 oz. extra spicy Bloody Mary mix
- I serrano or jalapeño chili pepper, to serve

Combine the dry spices and divide the mixture into two batches. Use one batch to rim an Old Fashioned glass, and put the other in a cocktail shaker along with the pineapple juice, rum, and Bloody Mary mix. Shake well. Serve over ice in your rimmed glass, and garnish with the chili pepper. You see how easy it is to follow instructions if you just take the time to listen???

I don't want to talk about it.

D espite what the police and your dad tell you, a person is never more vulnerable than when sitting in the pumpty-up chair of a new hairdresser. Think about it: there you are, roots exposed, covered in a tarp, offering up your shaggy, unwashed follicles to a scissor-wielding stranger. Worse yet, you will be relying on your dubious communication skills (thanks, honey, for pointing that out) to convey what it is you want this bored, underpaid dominatrix to do. What you don't understand is that she is only pretending to listen anyway; she only knows two different haircuts, and she is merely waiting for you to shut up so she can do a mental coin-flip. Stylists with a flair for the dramatic will rotate the chair away from the mirror as they work, distract you with gossip, and then whirl you around after the final snip has snapped. *Ta-∂aaaaa!* It would be great if, at that point, you could exclaim something positive or burst into applause, because, in her heart of hearts, she truly does want you to love it. (Love = big tip.) But what if you don't love it? Well, to be perfectly frank, if you're brazen enough to nuzzle your noggin into the Shampoo

Bowl of Fate, you're probably not the type to mince words. On the other hand, an even more brazen approach is to take the High Road: tell everyone you see that your askew new 'do is the very latest fad from Paris or Phuket or wherever. Crazy? Like a fox! I'll bet you a home perm that there's room for you in the Annals of Twentieth Century Fads. Some examples:

* Hairstyles were a big deal, literally speaking, in the early sixties. Trendy ladies favored the beehive, which was inspired by a tall, bulbous velvet hat. The beehive shape was achieved by backcombing (aka "ratting" or "teasing") most of the hair from ends to scalp, creating a sort of hair haystack, then smoothing the un-teased top layer over the bump. A large quantity of hairspray was applied to preserve the gravity-defiant shape, and often hairpins were needed for structural reinforcement. So labor-intensive was this hairstyle that women went to a great deal of trouble to preserve its integrity for as long as possible. They had to opt out of many carefree, mid-century American pastimes, such as swimming, riding in convertibles, and tickle fights. Pullover sweaters were relinquished to the attic. Sleeping had to be attempted with only a small pillow rolled up under the neck and the beehive itself wrapped in toilet paper and chiffon scarves. Kiss curls—those little flat spit curls at the temple and/or cheekbone— were finger-formed with a dollop of gel pomade and then taped to the face overnight. Why the effort? The higher the hair, the more tall and willowy the woman beneath it appeared. Starlets, socialites, and even our beloved First Lady Jackie Kennedy were fans.

* Dance marathons (aka bunion derbies) were popular in the 1920s and 1930s for two main reasons: (1) They provided folks with a diversion from the struggles of the Depression. (2) Contestants were given a roof over their head, at least for the duration of the marathon, and were fed twelve times per day. The downside is that dancers had to remain in motion forty-five minutes out of each hour. A contest could last several days, even weeks, until only one couple was left standing. In 1934, the American Social Hygiene Association (I wish I were kidding) began an investigation to determine the moral and humanitarian consequences of dance marathons. Their findings must have fizzled, however, because versions of dance marathons are still held to this day.

* Toga parties are attended by hundreds of thousands of college students each year. They are thought to have originated with National Lampoon's *Animal House*, where partygoers wrapped themselves in sheets and drank themselves into a bacchanalian stupor. But we actually owe Eleanor Roosevelt for throwing the very first US toga party; she was spoofing the pundits who were calling FDR "the second Caesar."

That's enough pop culture history for now. Let's get back to the delicious fad-in-the-making concoction at hand. Below Deck Rum is the highlight of this recipe, and I think it's one of the coolest things to happen to a Bloody Mary in a long time. Vodka, as you know, has been a staple ingredient in Bloodies for going on nine decades. Pepper-flavored vodka is a modern choice for those who want a bit more bang for their buck. However, it's not exactly the newest thing under the sun—ginger-flavored rum   is. Surprised? I was too. It delivers a different kind of sweet/spicy bite, doesn't scrimp on the heat factor, and is practically guaranteed to be the new kid on the Bloody Mary block. The pineapple juice in this particular recipe gives the ginger extra zing, but the homemade meat rub, both in the mix and on the rim, is what brings everything together and takes it downtown. Which is exactly where you ought to take your fad-tastic new haircut before you rip the poor stylist a new one. *C'est si bon!*

I Oughta Put a Big Carbon Footprint Right On Your Face, You SUV-Driving, Animal-Eating, Plastic-Wrapped, High-Fructose Son of a Bitch

Serves 6

6 lbs. fresh tomatoes
4 Tbsp. finely chopped red onion
1 red or green jalapeño pepper, chopped
4 Tbsp. chopped cucumber
Juice of 2 limes
2 Tbsp. soy sauce or Worcestershire sauce
    without anchovy
Salt, to taste (only if using Worcestershire sauce)
Freshly ground black pepper, to taste
Tabasco sauce, to taste
6 jiggers vodka
Celery stalks and lime quarters, to serve

To prepare the tomato juice, begin with very ripe, juicy tomatoes, and chop them coarsely. Place them in a stainless steel pot and bring them to a simmer over low heat. Cook until the tomatoes soften completely and their juices are released. Remove the pot from the heat, cool, and run the tomatoes through a food processor or juicer to remove the seeds and skin. Pour the tomato puree into a bowl and let it stand a half hour. If water rises to the top, skim off until it no longer does. Refrigerate immediately. When the tomato juice is well chilled, combine it with the remaining ingredients (minus the garnish) in a 2-quart pitcher. Place several ice cubes in 12-ounce glasses made out of windshields salvaged from the detritus associated with Hurricane Katrina, and fill with the Bloody Mary mix. Garnish each with a celery stalk and a lime quarter. Gather the tomato pulp, unused celery bits, and lime rinds for proper disposal. By this time tomorrow, you'll have the only 80-proof compost bin in the neighborhood.

I spent a fortune at the dry cleaner's getting the red paint out of this coat. Now that's what I call an inconvenient truth!

*U*h-oh, she's home. My neighbor and arch enemy. That's her right there, getting out of her Dodge Durango with that frosted hair and...oh my God, are those leather pants??? Yesterday I saw her walking out of a fast food place carrying a ginormous Coke and a McCarcass with fries. No, I swear. I was only there because we were picketing for PETA and I happened to see... Yeah, and she almost ran over my bike with her big stupid car. Look, look you guys, she's got about twelve plastic grocery bags! Ewww! Can you believe that? I bet even her boobs are made of plastic. She probably uses deodorant and shaves her legs too. Anyway, thanks for coming over to help me plan the spotted owl rally. Sorry my apartment's such a mess; I was gonna braid all this hemp into leashes for the Pygmy Goats for Orphans foundation, but I decided to go get another tattoo instead. I've got a special treat for you today. It's an all-natural, free-range, vegan, zero-greenhouse-gases Bloody Mary to start the day! I call it "Goin' Agro." No, no wait, how about "Kiss My Bumper Crop."

If you eschew anything that's canned, bottled, processed, frozen, or reconstituted, this recipe is for you. It's also a godsend for home gardeners who, after foisting tomatoes on neighbors, co-workers, delivery people, their Bunco group, their kids' teachers, and everyone at the dog park (including the dogs), are still left with a bewildering surplus. It's bursting with fresh, organic, self-righteous yumminess you just can't get off the shelf. It punches your "green" card, so don't punch the next ozone-depleting ignoramus that crosses your path. I first encountered a version of this Bloody Mary at an engagement party for a couple of zealous environmental advocates. The young man proposed with an antique solitaire ring so that there was no chance it could be a blood diamond. The pair wanted to be married in a barn and then afterward, rather than a tropical honeymoon, they planned to be off to the Arctic to catalogue habitats of harbor seals. The bride-to-be refused a traditional nuptial shower; instead, she invited her friends to a discussion group to raise awareness for starving children in Botswana. And the bachelor party? The fellas donated blood and then knocked back a few glasses of orange juice. Did I mention the blushing bride bought a recycled gown made of wood pulp? I didn't have the nerve to tell those two that the Bloody Mary was the best part of the fete. If you're planning an event for a back-to-nature crowd, this is the one to serve. Not only is it undeniably the most politically correct thing to come out of a liquor cabinet, but you can do all the prep work ahead of time so you can actually spend time with your guests. Here are a few other tips to help your group feel the love:

1. Hop on your bike and ride down to the co-op. Pick up some organic, sprouted whole grain bread. When you get it home, cut it into thinly sliced triangles, no crust. Brush a little olive oil on each piece, and top with farmer's cheese (or that leftover cheese from Urban Gleaners that's still in the Westfalia's fridge). Broil until bubbly.

2. Go out into your yard and gather up some fennel, mint, sage, and anything still in bloom. Arrange them in a vase for a great-smelling centerpiece.

3. Wear anything as long as it has a slogan. "Animals die to keep your fat ass alive" is a strong choice. Clothing made from bamboo or hemp is also appropriate, though too subtle for some.

4. For music, provide guests with small drums or gourds.

5. Rinse out your collection of Tibetan singing bowls, unless you have proper glassware. Bandanas make cute yet unfrivolous napkins.

When your get-together is over, collect all food scraps for the compost bin. Make a donation to www.carbonfund.org to offset the electricity you used in the kitchen. If your guests liked the Bloody Marys a little too much, drive them home in the Westie. How about you? Feel the global warming in your soul starting to calm down? I think Mary just found your Qi spot.

My Kids Found My "Private Drawer"

Serves 1

- 1 shot Grey Goose Le Citron vodka
- 1 shot sake
- 1 tsp. wasabi
- 6 oz. tomato juice
- 1 tsp. dried ginger powder
- 1 tsp. soy sauce
- 1 tsp. lime juice
- Fresh cilantro, to serve

Shake and strain all the ingredients (except the cilantro) into a Collins glass with ice. Garnish with cilantro and drink away the memory of what just happened.

My eyes! I have to boil my eyes!

D on't be fooled by Hollywood's current crop of Yummy Mummies who persist in cavorting around the planet in private jets and size 0 Balenciaga gowns. Everything changes when you have a child. *Everything.* Say goodbye to sleeping late. Quiet car rides. Your waistline. Leisurely dinners. Your libido. Privacy. Newborns are one thing, but a kid old enough to walk, talk, and rummage through your belongings is another problem altogether. At a certain age, kids have a vague understanding of what sex is and why it is. They deduce that their parents have "done it" at least once per offspring. As gross and unbelievable as that mental picture is, it doesn't hold a candle to finding a Polaroid of Mom or Dad in *flagrante delicto.* Or discovering a battery-powered plaything. Or your director's cut, wide-screen copy of *Spectator Pump.* People, I can't stress this enough: the way to avoid this kind of mortification is to keep your nightstand age-appropriate. Let me give you some examples.

Nightstands Through the Years

Single gals: Alarm clock set for 5 AM spinning class; remote control for TV and Wii; framed photos of dog, boyfriend, and both together; iPod dock; ethnic ceramic jar containing condoms; *Cosmopolitan* magazine.

Newlyweds: Alarm clock set for 6 AM breakfast in bed together before work; remote controls for TV, DVD, Blu-ray, and TiVo, all of which are still in boxes; framed wedding photo; bottle of Astroglide; current issue of *The Nest;* brushed nickel Crate & Barrel reading lamp.

New parents: Silenced alarm clock, since you're not sleeping anyway; baby monitor; digital camera with 4 GB of baby photos on the card; breast pump; dog-eared copy of *What To Expect When You're Expecting*, tube of Desitin.

Ten years later: Alarm clock set for 7 AM safety patrol duty; universal remote control with parental discretion feature enabled; framed t-ball, soccer, gymnastics, and dance recital photos; *Parents Magazine;* a pink plastic barrette; Victoria's Secret catalogs (on Daddy's side of the bed).

Middle age: Alarm clock set for 8 AM staff meeting; remote control with only six large buttons on it; framed photos of grandkids; Viagra; reading glasses; snore control nasal strips; Sudoku book.

Old age: Alarm clock that projects 24-inch-tall numbers onto the ceiling; denture glass; hearing aids; CPAP machine; framed photo of family reunion with everyone's name written on the back; liniment; coupon for Depends; book of crossword puzzles; heating pad.

But back to the situation at hand. Now suppose you, regardless of your age group, like to occasionally dip your hand in the proverbial nookie jar. And because you are chronically deprived of time, sleep, and privacy, you sometimes need a little help from a

Marital Aid. Your progeny do not need to know any of this. They don't even want to know. For heaven's sake, don't allow your night-stand to look like a one-night stand. Do everyone a favor and get rid of the evidence! Hide it. Burn it. Eat it. If you don't, you run the risk of being found out. By the entire neighborhood. Imagine the show-and-tell tomorrow at school! Your cheeks will be aflame with embarrassment for days, and you will momentarily consider seppuku to mitigate your shame. But here's an alternative to dis-embowelment that just may do the trick. This drink may very well be how "Mary" earned her "Bloody."

* It's got enough firepower to absolve even the deepest, darkest blot on your parental report card. At least it will take your mind off the debacle at hand.

* Scarlet letter, scarlet face, scarlet drink...it's a theme.

* The Asian-ness of the sake, wasabi, and soy sauce salute a culture wherein, if you want to get your freak on, you go to a love hotel. That way, the children can't see, hear, or smell a thing.

* One taste will cause you to flap your jowls about for a minute or so before any words come out, which will buy you time until you think up something to say. That's another edge the Yummy Mummies have over you: rather than trying to debrief the youngsters themselves, they simply have their publicists release a statement.

Don't worry. You did nothing wrong. Come to think of it, your kids should be the ones explaining why they were snooping in the first place. You just relax and enjoy that drink. Then call a locksmith.

GARNISH

The Bloody Mary Hall of Flame

The following recipes are only for the very adventurous among you. Repeat after me: "I, _____, do not hold Judy Bennett liable for the consequences of my decision to bring one of these Bloody Marys to Bob's retirement potluck."

Flaming Bloody Mary
Take any recipe that suits your fancy, and make it the usual way—only use a sturdy, unbreakable mug. Float an ounce or so of Bacardi 151 on top, then poke a piece of string into the drink so that half of it is submerged and half of it is hanging out. A two- or three-inch piece should be sufficient. When you are ready to serve, light the string on fire.

Bloody Mary Salad
Dissolve 1 package of lemon gelatin in 1 cup of hot tomato juice. Cool, then add 1 ounce of vodka, 1 tablespoon of lemon juice, a 1/2 teaspoon of Worcestershire sauce, and a 1/4 teaspoon of Tabasco sauce. Pour the mixture into 6 parfait glasses and put them in the fridge to set. You can really go crazy on the garnishes here; after all, it IS a salad. Pickled green beans, okra, asparagus, different kinds of peppers, stuffed green olives, prawns, pepperoni, cocktail onions, you name it.

Upside-Down Bloody Mary
Stand with your back to the bar. Bend over backwards so that your head is hanging upside down. Have a friend pour a shot of vodka and a shot of Bloody Mary mix into your mouth all at once. Stand up and swallow. This is a popular hangover cure, not only because of the Bloody Mary-ness of it but drinking it upside down forces blood to your head.

Bloody Mary Jane
Steep marijuana in tomato juice and a little vodka for two hours, then use it as a mixer in your favorite recipe. You'll want LOTS of garnish.

Bloodless Mary
Follow one of the more traditional recipes, but leave out the tomato juice completely.

Bleeding Mary
Another riff on the traditional mixture: don't add any tomato juice, and use equal amounts of Tabasco sauce and vodka.

Inside-Out Bloody Mary
Fill an old-school ice cube tray with Bloody Mary mixer and freeze until solid. Put several cubes in a glass, and then add your vodka, lemon juice, Tabasco sauce, and garnish.

PART IV

Affirmations

We have been serving tomato juice cocktails in our family for a number of years and consider them both delicious and valuable to our health.
   —Henrietta, 103 years old

This section is dedicated to the power of positive thinking. It's about self-love through believing you deserve good things and rewarding yourself when you have them. You'll find that these Bloody Marys are their own reward.

It's My Birthday and I Want Breakfast in Bed

Serves 1

4–5 dashes Worcestershire sauce
1 jigger vodka
Several dashes each of salt, celery salt,
    black pepper
2 dashes Tabasco sauce
3 oz. top-quality tomato juice
1–2 kumquats

Shake the first five ingredients with ice, and strain into an Old Fashioned glass. Garnish with the kumquats on a skewer and a generous helping of decadence.

Breakfast in bed was amazing,
but this pony ride blows.

You do so much for people. You work your fingers to the bone at your job. You gallantly maneuver through rush-hour traffic to accommodate the arrogant, the indecisive, and the just plain stupid. At home, you're the cook, housekeeper, nanny, secretary, chauffeur, valet, dog trainer, pediatrician, interior designer, travel agent, psychiatrist, gardener, provocateur, courier, life coach, event planner, mediator, fashion coordinator, and accountant. If and when you get a day off, it's usually a holiday. But the purpose of a holiday isn't for you to put your feet up and take it easy; they're for putting somebody else on a pedestal for the day. Think about it. Presidents Day. Veterans Day. Christmas. Wouldn't it be great if there were a holiday that was All About You? Well, good news, precious, because there is: your birthday. Just think! You can do whatever you want, whenever you want, as many times as you want, all that hallowed day.

Now before you pick up the phone to order that mink bed jacket you've had your eye on, there is one little fly in the ointment. You've got to call in sick to work.

Contrary to popular belief, you don't actually have to pretend to sound sick. I've prepared some excuses for you to choose from, one of which is guaranteed to fly with your particular boss and won't require you to take acting lessons ahead of time.

My grandmother died. Please note that this will only work if you are under the age of sixty. Your colleagues will most likely have never met your Nana, and there is very little chance of any of them running into her in the future. Bonus: if Nana lives (lived) out of town, you can wrangle a few extra days off for travel to and from the funeral.

My pet is sick. This is a good one because animals do develop rather alarming symptoms in a short amount of time. Then, of course, you have to take poor little Ignats to the vet, and then spend the remainder of the day giving him pills hidden in tiny pieces of cheese.

I have an optometrist appointment. Everyone knows that you can't get in to see the eye doctor before 8:30 or 9 in the morning, so don't feel you have to call in at the crack of dawn. When you do, just say it's a routine exam so you won't be asked to list your symptoms. Call back in a couple of hours and tell your boss you can't possibly drive to work with your eyes dilated, so you're taking the rest of the day off. If by chance you've recently been to the optometrist for real, you won't get away with saying you're going again. The next best thing is to announce that your appointment is with the gynecologist. You can still use the dilation excuse for staying home the rest of the day.

I have to wait for the plumber / cable guy / furnace repairman. Any of these could have sprung up without warning and can easily take all day to deal with. Be sure to remember which one you chose so you can keep your story straight tomorrow.

I must have food poisoning. Trust me, *no one* is going to ask you to describe what's going on. Those who have had it know all too well, and the rest will just be too grossed out to hear it.

Now that the unpleasant part is out of the way, fluff your pillows and get ready to enjoy this luscious little Bloody Mary. It's subtle, which means you'll be sober enough to enjoy Your Special Day any way you want. It's light, so it can accompany your meal without trying to *be* your meal. It's basic, therefore you don't need to leave your cozy little nest to run all over tarnation in search of ingredients. It's delicious, meaning not too spicy, not too salty, not too anything. Juuuuust right. Think of it as the present you got yourself. And I can't think of anyone more deserving, can you? (Your secret's safe with me.)

This Outfit and I Deserve a Night on the Town

Serves 1

1 jigger vodka
1 dash celery salt
2 dashes original Tabasco sauce
2 dashes green Tabasco sauce
1/2 tsp. cream-style horseradish, or to taste
1 tsp. A-1 steak sauce
2 dashes Worcestershire sauce (preferably Lea & Perrins)
1 lemon wedge
1 lime wedge
46-oz. bottle premium tomato juice
Garnish: celery, lemon wedge, lime wedge, green olive, dill
    pickle spear, pepperoncini, sport pepper, cherry pepper,
    and whatever else catches your eye (optional)

Mix together the first seven ingredients with ice in a cocktail shaker until cold, and strain into a pint glass. Squeeze all the juice from the lemon and lime wedges into the glass and fill the rest of the space with tomato juice. Now, garnish like your drink deserves a night out as well! I suggest a celery stalk (the longer and more ostentatious the better) alongside a skewer or two containing most if not ALL of the garnishes listed above. "No thanks, I'm full" is not in your vocabulary tonight, hot stuff.

Don't you just LOVE casual Friday?

A recipe that calls for dashing, shaking, and squeezing demands a certain kind of mojo. And I can tell just from looking at you that you've got plenty to spare. What's different about you? Have you lost a couple of pounds? Been on vacation? Did you get some last night? Wait a sec, I know what it is. That outfit is killer!

I used to be the kind of girl who, given a hundred dollars, would gleefully scour the clearance racks and come home with twenty items that cost five dollars each. I believed quantity was the path to versatility. And if one of those items had a laundry mishap, went out of style, or reminded me of a person I'd rather forget, into the rag pile it would go without hesitation; I had plenty more to take its place. This past year, though, I had a sartorial epiphany.

I was walking along the road, minding my own business, wearing a pair of (too short? cropped!) mom jeans that I found at a going-out-of-business sale, and an itchy polyester blouse with plastic buttons. On my feet were used (not by me) vinyl sandals that were a half-size too small but only cost two dollars. I was carrying an imitation Kate Spade clutch that was free for hosting a Purses By Design party at my house. Suddenly, out of nowhere, there was this really bright light. The voice of my stylist, Kymm, boomed from the heavens. "My God, why would you go out in public like that? That's so *wrong*." She said I should continue along the road until I came to the city, then I would know what to do. Blinded like I was from the light, it wasn't easy to find my way to the city, but I followed the smell of Jean Patou and trust fund money to my destination: Sak's. I had always held the impression of such establishments as stuffy, matronly, and decidedly unsexy. But, guided by the edict from my wise and powerful stylist, through the beveled doors I went. I soon found myself standing in the shell-pink dressing room wearing a five-thousand-dollar Dolce and Gabbana suit. The scales fell from my eyes and I was reborn. I felt elegant! Beautiful! Omnipotent! And lemme-hear-an-amen, sexy! Never again would I persecute these hallowed halls. Target, I renounce thee!

Here's the moral of the story: Clothes don't make the (wo)man, but surrounding yourself with sights, sounds, textures, smells, and flavors that please you can send your outlook on life into the stratosphere. Take the time to seek out the best quality you can afford. You'd be surprised what a difference there is between two hundred and four hundred thread count. Folgers vs. Peet's. Glade Plugins vs. a dozen fresh pink roses in a sparkling crystal vase. Get it?

Ordinary people can drink ordinary Bloody Marys. Not you. You're about to elevate your Bloody Mary experience to match your sublime new outfit that cost you a month's pay. Start with the vodka. Contrary to logic and popular opinion, vodkas are not all alike. Each brand has a distinct smell, flavor, aftertaste, and degree of smoothness. That's because different brands use different distilling methods and ingredients, such as wheat, rye, beets, corn, potatoes, sugarcane, and even hemp seeds. Tell the folks at the liquor store your mission, and ask them what they would recommend. Stay away from any trendy flavors here, and don't be swayed by a cool label or marketing hype. More expensive doesn't always equate to better flavor.

The next detail to pay attention to is the tomato juice. Browse the juice aisle at a specialty market and look at the list of ingredients on the bottles. If there are things in there that you can't pronounce or have never heard of, they probably don't belong in your Bloody Mary. In my experience, Knudsen tomato juice tastes fresh-on-the-vine authentic; Campbell's makes a nice product for the money too. On the other hand, some people swear by the cheaper stuff. It tends to be watery, which allows your secondary ingredients to shine. To each her own. This is your day; you make the call.

Lastly, the garnish. Splurge on the crunchiest celery. The fattest olive. The tangiest pickle. The hottest pepper. The juiciest lemon and lime. Then dash, shake, and squeeze your way into that outfit. And let the good times roll!

This Is My First Really Healthy Relationship

Serves 2

Several dashes salt and black pepper
1 jigger vodka
2 tsp. garlic powder
2 tsp. lemon pepper
1 tsp. horseradish
2 Tbsp. Worcestershire sauce
8 oz. high-quality tomato juice
1 fresh lemon, cut in wedges, to serve
Several pickled asparagus spears, to serve

Rim two Old Fashioned glasses with the salt and pepper in equal measure. Combine the remaining ingredients (minus the lemon and asparagus) in a cocktail shaker. Strain and pour over ice cubes in the prepared glasses, and garnish each with a lemon wedge and asparagus. Here's to love!

He had me at "Dollface."

I've invented a card game called "Relationships," and it can be played by as many people as you want. The way it works is simple: the more diamonds you give away, the more hearts you get back. If you run out of diamonds, you might find yourself on the receiving end of a club. Be cautious about giving your hearts away to just anybody. And don't even think about giving a club to someone who's expecting diamonds! You'll be ejected from the room in spades.

That used to be me. After far too many years filled with jokers and wild cards, I've finally found someone who's playing with an unmarked deck. After all those years of kissing frogs, kissing ass, and kissing my self-respect goodbye, I'm finally having an honest-to-goodness, drama-free, grown-up relationship. Boring? Not on your life. In fact, I discovered that a solid foundation built of compatibility, respect, and shared values is the best aphrodisiac around. And, being in a good emotional place opens the floodgates for the universe to bestow all of its many blessings.

(It doesn't hurt that this man, besides being my best friend, soul mate, and accomplice, is also hotter than a three-dollar pistol.)

One of the things we agreed upon early in our marriage was to strive for excellence in all things. It's how we prioritize everything from getting dressed to go out, to choosing bathroom tile, to how we will spend a lazy Saturday afternoon. We don't always go for the most ostentatious, expensive, *au courant* tidbit on the proverbial dessert tray, but whatever it is, it must be well-designed, purposeful, and aesthetically fabulous. What this does is create a delicious romantic bubble around the two of us, like we are the custodians of a rare and treasured object (which is true). We've both been in relationships where one person or the other always seemed to be chasing the next shiny toy, but for selfish, divisive reasons. Never again. Power struggles are fine in Strip Jenga, but otherwise they are not part of our *modus operandi*.

This Bloody Mary is a wonderful example of what I'm talking about. It's devoid of any bells and whistles. The ingredient list is based on a classic, if predictable, formula that's been trusted for three generations. It delivers on its promises, even exceeds expectations, but not in a be-careful-what-you-wish-for way. The garlic and horseradish bond seamlessly together without competing for dominance, and the lemon pepper gives it a fresh, modern edge. No games, no drama, no fooling. One tip: no generic, dented-can, bargain-basement tomato juice. Shop around for the really good stuff. The same goes for your condiments. Become well-acquainted with the purveyors of your local specialty or gourmet store to get timely, mistake-proof information.

Take some advice from the girl who spent way too many years playing Go Fish: tricks are for kids. Elegant, timeless perfection feeds your soul. Tonight, I want you to pull out your Michael C. Fina glasses, whip up a couple of quintessential Bloody Marys, and lay all your cards on the table. Show your lover just how committed you are to making this the best relationship the two of you have ever had. These are the items you should have at the ready.

* A smokin' outfit in his favorite color and show-stopping dainties underneath.

* Soft background music (bonus: a recording of a concert you attended together or the CD you listened to on a romantic drive).

* Bite-sized treats that you can feed each other with your fingers. There are lots of good choices out there, but gravitate toward things that melt in your mouth (loud crunching or marathon chewing can be deal breakers). Think strawberries, soft cheeses, tiny empanadas, the asparagus spear from your Bloody Mary.

* Almond oil, for backrub purposes. If your slippery activities go further than that, put down a plastic shower curtain first. You don't want to leave an embarrassing stain on your Aubusson rug.

Relationships are a lot like Bloody Marys. If they're too hot to handle, they're fun for a while but eventually burn themselves out. When you find a good one, treasure it and it will pay you back a hundredfold.

My High School Reunion is Five Pounds and Two Weeks Away

Serves 1

> 3 oz. tomato juice
> Dash each fresh lemon juice, Worcestershire sauce,
>   and Tabasco sauce
> 1 fresh lime wedge
> (No booze in this one, ladies and gentlemen!)

Pour the tomato juice and seasonings over ice in a chilled Old Fashioned glass, and garnish with the lime. Practice holding the Bloody Mary in one hand, while you fondle the tanned arm flesh of your Diesel-underwear-model date with the other.

What are YOU looking at?
I'm big-boned, all right?

W ow. It's been ten years, three kids, fifteen pounds, two bad knees, and a heap of wrinkles since you last saw any of the old gang. Ever since that crimson and gold postcard showed up in the mail, you've been thinking about what to wear, what to say, who to bring, and above all, how you're going to manage to hold your stomach in for three hours straight. Not to worry. I've got your game plan right here.

Diet: Fact #1: Researchers from Arizona State University found that the vitamin C in citrus fruit, particularly lemons, is directly related to the body's ability to burn fat for fuel. The more vitamin C in your diet, the more efficiently you metabolize fat.

Fact #2: Drinking tomato juice before a meal can trick your body into feeling satiated, and you'll wind up eating less.

Fact #3: Alcohol is really just sugar, adding sixty-four empty calories per ounce to whatever you're drinking. Besides, its disinhibitory effect can cause you to throw caution to the wind and overindulge at the buffet table.

Fact #4: This slimmed-down version of the Bloody Mary you already love is going to be your new BFF.

Exercise: A regular walking program of just thirty minutes three to five times per week is enough to trigger weight loss, tone your muscles, and give your skin a healthy glow. To make your workouts more fun, try this Blast from the Past playlist on your iPod. Or to really get in the mood, make yourself a mix tape and pop it in your Walkman.

> "Livin' On a Prayer," by Bon Jovi
> "Any Way You Want It," by Journey
> "Footloose," by Kenny Loggins
> "YMCA," by The Village People
> "Call Me," by Blondie
> "Beautiful Day," by U2
> "The Boys of Summer," by Don Henley
>
> And for the cool down:
> "Right Here Waiting," by Richard Marx
> "Where Does My Heart Beat Now,"
>   by Celine Dion

Other: One word—Spanx.

* Fact: Tomatoes are rich in lycopene, which is a powerful antioxidant. Twice a week, try a Lightening, Brightening, Tightening Bloody Mary Facial. In a glass dish, mix together 2 tablespoons of celery salt, 1 tablespoon of tomato juice, and the juice of 1 lemon. Spread gently all over your face, neck, and decolletage. Also works on rough elbows, knees, and heels. Wait five minutes, then rinse off. Follow with moisturizer.

* Lemons are a terrific, natural way to fight bad breath. Suck on a wedge, if you can do it without crying, or chew on a piece of the rind.

Last but not least: don't sweat it. It's really not all about you. Ten years has passed for everyone in the room, dear heart, not just you. But if you follow these steps, including a regular dose of this slimming, age-fighting Bloody Mary, you're sure to be the most radiant one there.

Hos Before Bros

Serves 1

2 shots vodka
6 oz. tomato juice
1/4 tsp. celery salt
1/4 tsp. cinnamon
1 dash black pepper
1–2 dashes cayenne pepper
1 dash salt
1/4 tsp. Tabasco sauce
1/2 tsp. Worcestershire sauce
1 blue-cheese-stuffed green olive,
    to serve (optional)

Measure all the ingredients into a cocktail shaker, and then pour over ice in a Collins glass. Garnish with an olive if you've got it. If not, dispatch one of the hovering gentlemen to the nearest store.

Mom! Ralph's spying on our girls-only club again.
And make him take off that dress!

Wilma had Betty. Lucy had Ethel. Laverne had Shirley. They shared secrets, advice, recipes, adventure, and laughter, and knew more about each other than the men in their lives did. And when the fecal matter really hit the fan, whom did they reach out to? That's right, not their parents, not their boss, not a sexy stranger in a bar. Behold the power of the BFF.

About four or five times a week, I get an e-mail that contains a cute and uplifting story poking fun at my ever-increasing age, girth, forgetfulness, and the like. Toward the end it always says, "Send this to twelve friends, including me, within the next fifteen minutes and something truly amazing will happen in your life." Do men send e-mails like that to *their* friends? Hah! Don't be ridiculous. Men couldn't care less about uplifting each other unless it takes place on a playing field of some kind. Besides, did you ever know a man to successfully accomplish a task under a tight deadline? Truly amazing life event be damned! He'll forward it when Bella and Edward from *Twilight* decide to take up sunbathing. (Okay, the truth? I only forward them because my friends and I think they're funny, not because I'm being coerced to do so. Don't judge!)

More reasons why women are better than men:

1. Women can endure more discomfort, for longer periods of time. (Like anyone gave us a choice.)

2. Women have more and better orgasms. Or we have the ability to pretend we do.

3. Women are good tactical opponents in business, politics, finance, and everything else because their brains are on the inside, not poking out of a bathrobe.

4. Women don't give each other wedgies, pass gas at will, punch their friends in the arm as hard as they can, scratch their genitals in public, or shout at the TV (unless it's the Home Shopping Network or *The Biggest Loser*).

Don't take your BFF for granted another day. Show her how much she means to you by handing her this extra-special, never-let-you-down, wind-beneath-my-wings Bloody Mary. Like a true friendship, its flavors are comfortingly familiar. All the basics you've come to depend on are there: vodka, tomato, celery salt, black pepper, Tabasco sauce, Worcestershire sauce. But don't stop there. Throw in the cinnamon for all the Thanksgiving dinners you've eaten together. For being on a first-name basis with each other's moms. For taking care of her dog when she went to the Bahamas. For every time she picked up your kids from school when you were sick. Now add the cayenne. Add one dash if you've ever double-dated. Add two dashes if you went home with each other's date that night. Add more if you man-swap on a regular basis. When you feel like you have a mixture that does your relationship justice, pour it into a tall glass, plop an olive on top, and present it to your pal like the queen that she is.

Be sure to make a Bloody Mary for yourself while you're at it. Because if you've got a friend this terrific, chances are you're not such a bad egg yourself.

The More Resentment I Release, the More Love I Can Express

Serves 1

- 3 oz. Spicy Hot V8
- 3 oz. Clamato
- 1 pinch horseradish
- 1 dash Worcestershire sauce
- 1 dash Tabasco sauce
- 1 tsp. olive brine
- 1 pinch celery salt
- 1 pinch black pepper
- 1 jigger vodka
- 1 lemon or lime wedge, to serve
- 1 cocktail onion, to serve
- 1 garlic-stuffed green olive, to serve

Excluding the last three ingredients, combine the remainder in a highball glass and stir. Garnish with the lemon (or lime), cocktail onion, and olive stabbed by—er, threaded on—a skewer.

Hey, Arthur, remember that Ex-lax brownies incident with your mother? It WASN'T an accident.

I have a special corner in my house with a prayer rug, a candle, and a stack of Melody Beattie books. I go there whenever I need to rediscover my true purpose and quell any thoughts that cause disharmony within my spirit.

You see, my family is wacked.

On one hand, they are the reason I know what I know about drinking. "Likker" is their means for telling time ("It's gotta be five o'clock somewhere!"), their entertainment ("Let's get the dog drunk!"), and their primary topic of conversation ("How was your drive home last night? Man, you were *hammered*!"). Their influence made me who I am today: an otherwise well-adjusted woman who is obviously preoccupied with Bloody Marys. On the other hand, with a few notable exceptions (and you know who you are!), my kith and kin are dismissive, manipulative, and un-scrupulous. (Oh, don't look so scandalized. The family members I'm referring to will never read this, or any other book for that matter. None of them even own bookshelves, because if they did, where would the rifle rack go?)

Just a minute. I'm going to pay a little visit to my Happy Place. Resentments are like canker sores. Anyone can get them, and they can attack from out of nowhere. If you ignore resentments and hope they'll go away, that only makes them bigger. What you have to do is confront them, and the quicker you do, the sooner you can heal and get on with the rest of your life. Experts offer several handy remedies to try when you just need to blow off a little steam: walking, deep breathing, yoga, and meditation. But I forget about those things when I'm righteously pissed off, don't you? The Good Book says to turn the other cheek. The AA Big Book says if you pray for the person you resent, you will be free. Friedrich Nietzsche's book, *The Anti-Christ*, says that resentment is born of human beings' innate will to power, and is thus unavoidable. Judy's book says it's high time for a Bloody Mary! And here are the steps on *that* path to enlightenment:

1. Take a deep, cleansing breath and ponder how the need to be right often overrides the need for peace. As you do this, put all the drink ingredients into the glass in no particular order. Notice how nicely they coexist. One is no more or less vital to the whole than another. Silently forgive those who are too stupid to realize how unimportant they are.

2. Take a long-handled spoon or a swizzle stick and stir the mixture together. You may not be in control of how people treat you, but you are by-god in control of stirring this drink to within an inch of its life. By the time your wrist starts aching, you will begin to feel calmer.

3. Take a sip. Focus your awareness on how each flavor contributes to the whole without upsetting the balance. All are necessary. It's spicy, true, but

mellowed by the savory roundness of the Clamato and the olive brine. It's got enough grit to be taken seriously, enough clarity to be refreshing, and just enough alcohol to take the edge off your mood without plunging you into a full-blown pity party. Repeat your affirmation about releasing resentment with every sip.

4. If the resentment is so huge that you cannot forgive, practice mindful and deliberate forgetfulness. Trick yourself into not remembering the details of whatever's eating you, and watch your resentment melt away. To pull this one off, you might need another Bloody Mary or two. Repeat as needed.

Will the Real Bloody Mary Please Stand Up?

Cocktails. Movie titles. Comic book heroines. Urban legends. What next? Did you know that there are and have been real, live, flesh-and-blood women walking around named Bloody Mary? It's true. And they are as endlessly fascinating and larger-than-life as their liquid counterparts.

1. Ask anyone in New Orleans who the number one expert on voodoo is, and they'll tell you it's Bloody Mary. Voodoo queen, shaman, healer, storyteller, historian, medium, lightworker, psychic, and ghost hunter, she also happens to be descended from another famous Bloody Mary, Queen Mary I (see below). She has appeared on The History Channel, A&E, and CNN. Visitors to The Big Easy say her Tour of the Undead is not to be missed. She can even perform weddings. (www.bloodymarystours.com)

2. Three young ladies in Prague started a zine known as *Bloody Mary* to spread feminist ideals in the Czech Republic. They claim the name came to them by accident, because they were originally talking about drinks, but later realized that it was pretty symbolic: Bloody Mary was the nickname of Queen Mary I of England (yes, her again), and it is also suggestive of menstruation. The group formed in 2000 and has since added another member. The Bloody Mary Collective, as they call it, raises money by

organizing concerts and feminist parties, making t-shirts, and publishing the zine.

3. Here, finally, is the skinny on Mary I of England. In her religious zeal against the Protestants, she ordered more than three hundred of her countrymen burned at the stake. If this wasn't enough to earn her whispered nickname "Bloody Mary," rumor had it that she terminated a number of her pregnancies so as not to introduce an heir into her Protestant lineage. It is also said that the nursery rhyme "Mary, Mary, Quite Contrary" is about her attempts to establish Catholicism as the national religion.

4. Queen Ranavalona I of Madagascar has been called, among other unflattering things, The Bloody Mary of Madagascar. Her claim to fame is the death by torture of nearly half of her subjects between 1828 and 1861. It seems she was fanatical about abolishing Christianity in her kingdom. But wait, it gets better. Ranavalona was the adopted daughter of King Andrianampoinimerina, or as his personal shopper called him, Ramalamadingdong. When he died, his eldest son, Radama I, assumed the throne, but not for long. Ranavalona poisoned the new king, and before word could get out about his death, she ordered all his potential successors captured. She took the throne unopposed. But wait, there's still more. She gave birth to a son, Prince Rakoto, claiming that her ex-king / adoptive brother / murder victim Radama was the father, AND gave birth to him more than nine months after she offed the alleged daddy.

5. Bloody Mary #4 of the Texas Rollergirls' team, the Hell Marys, is better known at Our Lady of Perpetual Forgiveness as Mary Grace Margaret Catherine O'Brien. She plays two positions, jammer and blocker. (Father Florencio might have more to say about that after a glass or two of communion wine!) Originally from Rochester, New York, this is what she says makes her blood boil: "Hail Marys, cheap vodka, anything pink." *Austin Fit Magazine* held a competition to find the ten fittest athletes in town, and our Mary was selected. She says in her blog, "Kudos to Austin Fit for recognizing that athleticism and fishnet stockings are not mutually exclusive." (www.txrollergirls.com)

6. The multitalented though unfortunately named Bobbie Weiner is the Bloody Mary of Hollywood, and the mascot of US military forces at home and abroad. Best known for her makeup artistry, particularly in the movies *Titanic* and *Behind Enemy Lines*, she is 20th Century Fox's makeup consultant, and she uses her own products on the set. A few years ago, Bobbie was given the Defense Department's Gold Medal for the quality of her camouflage face paint. She has developed an eponymous line of Halloween makeup, sports fan makeup, funeral home makeup (The Final Touch), hot sauce, Bloody Mary mix, and even a comic book. In fact, you can see the image of the Bloody Mary comic book character emblazoned on the noses of the military's Black Hawk helicopters and their rocket pods. "The comic book premises

are all about helping people, being a good person, and not asking anything for just being who you are." She says the crew of her first movie, *Pumpkinhead II*, dubbed her Bloody Mary, "and it has stuck since then." (www.dearbloodymary. com)

PART V

Destinations

Tomatoes and oregano make it Italian; wine and tarragon make it French; lemon and cinnamon make it Greek; soy sauce makes it Chinese; garlic makes it good.
  —Alice May Brock, author

Certain flavors or scents have the power to transport you to places far, far away...places you have visited, dream of visiting, or that exist only in your imagination. The Bloody Marys you are about to meet have such powers. They are the best *stay*-cation of all. They are affordable, versatile, able to be embarked upon at the drop of a hat, and can be enjoyed alone or with chosen companions. And the best part? You are not only allowed to bring all the liquids your heart desires in your carry-on, it's required. You're going to love the playful combinations of spices, unexpected alcohols, and inspired presentations. Your taste buds will want to dance naked in a fountain.

My Tax Refund Just Bought Me a Week in Cabo

Serves 1

2 shots premium tequila
6 oz. tomato juice, chilled
1 tsp. ground coriander
1 dash Tabasco sauce
Salt and black pepper, to taste
1 lemon slice
Pickled green beans, to serve

Mix the tequila and tomato juice in a pilsner glass filled with ice cubes. Add the coriander and Tabasco sauce, along with salt and black pepper to taste. Then squeeze and dunk the slice of lemon, stir, and serve, using the pickled green beans for garnish. (How do you say "Hot damn!" in Spanish?)

Hola, *fellas.*

April is the best month of the year in the Pacific Northwest. The weather clears up, tulips and daffodils are in bloom, daylight savings time begins, and insufferable pundits cluster in coffee shops to celebrate International Tiresome Wit Month. For a lucky few, April brings another kind of joy: their tax refund. For a very lucky few, the refund is large enough to pay for a trip to Topeka, Kansas, for National Hairball Awareness Day. Or if you're sufficiently aware of hairballs for the time being, and you'd enjoy a change in longitude and some well-deserved lassitude, you could head down to Cabo. This Bloody Mary is just the ticket to get you in the right frame of mind while you're still in the planning stages.

Once there, drinking in Mexico is simple: Don't use any water or ice because it may contain unfriendly bacteria. Ingesting or even brushing your teeth with poorly sanitized water can give you what is known as Montezuma's Revenge, the Gringo

Gallop, or the Tourist Two-Step. If you like your Bloody Mary ice-cold, you can keep your bottle of tequila in the freezer and the tomato juice in the fridge.

Preview some south-of-the-border flavors. It's hard to imagine Mexican food without cilantro. Coriander is just the dried seeds of the cilantro plant. You can buy coriander already ground, or get the seeds and grind them yourself. The taste is a little more pungent when freshly ground, even if it does require an extra step. Be sure to buy from a trusted source or you may have a different experience altogether (see above).

And speaking of these local flavors, Mexican nightspots are filled with nubile American teenagers doing body shots. I recommend *not* practicing with your special Cabo Bloody Mary. It is simply too big, and you will end up with red liquid (and "uncool") all over your face.

Use caution with the Tabasco sauce. Extra-spicy food, for those not used to it, is another sure-fire way to invite old Montezuma to the door of your *casita*. Start small, and by the time you actually get to your destination, you'll be able to guzzle hot sauce with the best of them.

Finally, you'll want a cocktail that assembles in seconds so you don't miss out on a minute of the fun. This Bloody Mary requires no blending, shaking, or aerating. Just throw it together and plunk in a straw. If you close your eyes, you can almost feel your toes in the sand now. Or did you step in some salt? That's what you get for dancing on the table.

Actually, I'm More of a Ski Lodge Bum

Serves 8

46 oz. V8
1/3 cup dry Italian salad dressing mix
Horseradish, to taste
2 cups vodka
8 celery stalks

Combine V8, salad dressing mix, and horseradish in a Crock-Pot, cover, and cook on high 1 to 2 hours. Serve in coffee mugs, with 2 shots of vodka in each and the celery stalks as a garnish. It almost makes you wish winter lasted a little bit longer.

Yay, we're here! Now could you point me to the hot tub?

When it comes to being outdoors, I'm strictly a fair weather girl. As a matter of fact, I'm normally cold anywhere I am. If people are standing around bare-limbed and saying, "Wow, can you believe how hot it is today?" I'm the one reaching for a parka. How I long for the day when I have my first hot flash! So as you might have guessed, I don't spend a great deal of time outdoors between November and March. But when I do, this Bloody Mary is the thing I look forward to when I return home. It works because it honors the basic principles of how to stay warm in cold weather:

* Experts say the trick to surviving low temperatures is to think about keeping heat in as opposed to keeping cold out. A steaming mug full of Bloody Mary will get some heat in you for sure.

To really turn up the ol' thermostat, add some more horseradish. Your entire GI tract will be toasty for hours. Maybe days.

* Start with warm, dry equipment. This certainly applies to mittens and boots, but what it really refers to is dry Italian salad dressing mix and a nice dry vodka. Preheating your mugs before pouring is a nice touch, and it's easy to do with just a swish of hot water.

* Move as much as possible. You've got an hour or two to kill while the Crock-Pot sizzles away and your friends are still on the slopes. Use your imagination. Dance, shadowbox, jump on the beds, practice Bond girl poses... No one is looking. Go crazy! Any or all of these tunes should get your metabolism racing.

> "Baby, It's Cold Outside," by Dean Martin
> "When the Night Turns Cold,"
>   by Tobias Froberg
> "Summertime in Wintertime,"
>   by Badly Drawn Boy
> "First Light's Freeze," by the Castanets
> "First Snow on Brooklyn," by Jethro Tull
> "The Longest Winter," by Pedro the Lion
> "Winter A-Go-Go," by Yo La Tengo
> "Cold & Wet," by Bonnie 'Prince' Billy
> "Shiver," by Coldplay
> "A Hazy Shade of Winter,"
>   by Simon & Garfunkel
> "Cold Water," by Damien Rice
> "Winter's Come and Gone," by Gillian Welch

"Cold As It Gets," by Patty Griffin
"Shiver Me Timbers," by Tom Waits
"Running On Ice," by Billy Joel

* Share body heat. Vodka makes you want to snuggle. Millions of Russians can't be wrong. That's why there are millions of Russians.

* The hungrier you are, the colder you'll feel. This is a hearty, filling drink, made more so by the warm and creamy consistency. And, you can eat your swizzle stick when you're done.

* Have a little nip of alcohol. There's a reason why St. Bernards carry casks of liquor to lost or injured mountaineers. (If you want the truth, being a vasodilator, alcohol actually makes hypothermia worse, but it makes you not care as much that you're freezing to death.)

This Bloody Mary will chase away your chills no matter where you find yourself. At home, it goes great with a fluffy omelette and whole wheat toast. Or pour it into a Thermos and take it fishing, hiking, skiing, or tramping through a Christmas tree lot in the pouring rain (that one's more my speed). It makes me warmer than my leopard-print Snuggie, and I'll take it over a hot flash any day.

I've Decided to Go Back to College

Serves 3 to 4

    20 oz. tomato juice
    1 tsp. cracked pepper
    2 Tbsp. HP sauce
    1 tsp. liquid aminos
    1 Tbsp. hot sauce
    2 Tbsp. soy sauce
    4 oz. gin
    3–4 pepperoncini, to serve
    3–4 pickled green beans, to serve

Stir the first seven ingredients together in a tall pitcher, and serve over ice cubes in highball glasses. Garnish with 1 pepperoncini and 1 green bean each. This recipe will help you brush up on your math and chemistry. See? You're practically an honor student already.

Introducing the University of Sculleryville varsity cheerleading squad!

If there's a bright spot to this crappy economy of ours, it's that it gives people a chance to reinvent themselves. Have you been secretly fantasizing about a career change? Now that you've been laid off and your company has outsourced your position to a country you've never even heard of, why not go back to school and do something you've always wanted to do? Don't worry about being too old. There are so many adults at the career change juncture nowadays that school cafeterias are offering senior discounts.

But what to study? Try to remember what you wanted to be when you grew up, and see if that career path has the same appeal now.

1. **Superhero**—They get to wear cool costumes and have superpowers, but they're on city payroll, so they don't make much money. People they rescue usually say, "How can I ever repay you?" but I

never see them actually do it. Superheroes tend to be loners and have trouble getting insurance.

2. **Firefighter**—Still a prestigious job and a decent wage, but the physical requirements put it out of reach for many people. It's more demanding than other public service jobs, largely due to the finesse required to slide down a cold brass pole at top speed (and bulkily clothed, I might add). Rescuing people can be a great way to meet eligible singles, however. Best of all: hazmat suits are surprisingly flattering on all body types.

3. **Princess**—This job requires a working knowledge of the country that you are the princess of, in case you are ever interviewed by Barbara Walters. It also requires having royal parents or the ability to forge documents that say you do. And there can be lots of travel involved. Princesses don't draw an actual paycheck, but that's okay; everything is given to them anyway.

4. **Professional athlete**—There is no age limit for this job (golfers, bowlers), but there will be specific fitness demands depending on the sport. You will also have to develop a knack for breaking the law or getting involved in sex scandals. The salary and notoriety is the same whether you are a great talent or a huge screw-up. After a while, you don't even have to compete anymore because you'll get rich doing product endorsements on TV.

5. **Butterfly**—Unless you plan to join Cirque du Soleil or the Diva Las Vegas Drag Queen Revue, I think you can let this one go.

6. **Race car driver**—This is an easy field to break into because you already know how to drive. And unlike pro athletes, you don't have to act like a spoiled, narcissistic delinquent to be famous. Buy extra medical, life, and car insurance well in advance of making your new career choice known, and trim down as much as you can. Why? Any extra weight in the car will slow you down; the cockpits are teeny-tiny; and the jumpsuits are unforgivably tight.

See? You've got tons of options. Go ahead, mix up a Bloody Mary and give it some thought. It will inspire you, because it's been reinvented too. Back in the 1920s, when Bloody Mary was born, she was just vodka and tomato juice. Nothing more, nothing less. Then in 1933, she made her official debut into womanhood with the addition of Worcestershire sauce, salt and pepper, hot sauce, and the like. As you can see, Mary, like Betty White, is no spring chicken. Yet she's taken a good look around lately and decided it's time to shake things up. After all, when you've been around as long as she has, you can do whatever the hell you want. HP sauce, aminos, soy sauce, and gin are not the ingredients of a young upstart. They are sophisticated, thoughtful, and creative. They comprise a Bloody Mary that has realized its childhood dreams. If Mary can do it, so can you! Old, schmold. When you get done cracking the pepper, get out there and crack a few books.

I Never Got to Go Backpacking Through Europe

Serves 1

2 oz. tomato juice
1 jigger Scotch whiskey
6 dashes Tabasco sauce
1 tsp. Worcestershire sauce
1/8 tsp. freshly ground black pepper
1 tsp. grated onion
1 rosemary sprig, to serve

Combine all the ingredients (except the rosemary) in a cocktail shaker with ice cubes; mix well. Strain into a pocket flask or bota bag. Crush or bruise the rosemary to release the flavors. Here's how: separate the leaves from the stem, then literally crush them with the back of a wooden spoon. Sprinkle several in for flavor. Rub the rest between your hands and run your fingers over any exposed skin. Rosemary makes a dandy insect repellant.

Faster, Jeffrey!
Can't you hear the ocean?

I had a few acquaintances at college who, by the age of eighteen, had taken themselves on some pretty amazing adventures. Not me. I was the sheltered kid of a couple of emotionally constipated *nouveau riche* parents. I thought Machu Picchu was an arcade game. My folks took me to Europe once, when I was in high school. It was one of those tour packages that cater to the over sixty-five crowd. The air-conditioned autobus made sure to hit all the predictable tourist attractions throughout England, France, and Italy, with lengthy stops at churches and souvenir stands. My school friends had very different travel experiences from mine. They talked about Eurail passes and hostels and street food. Summer music festivals in Budapest. Kinky parties in Amsterdam. Bedbugs. It all sounded incredibly exotic and cool.

I was going to put a trip together for the summer after my freshman year at Whitman, but I got engaged instead. The next summer, the engagement was off, but I landed a killer gig as a professional cheerleader. The summer after that, my mom was diagnosed with bladder cancer and I wanted to stay close to home.

I graduated the following year, and I just assumed I was supposed to bang out a resume, start a career, find an apartment, and all that stuff. I forgot all about the backpacking-through-Europe thing until my own kids went off to college. Now I'm too busy to go off on a lark of that magnitude. But ever since I discovered this Bloody Mary, I can experience the adventure any time I want, without ever leaving home. Want to learn how? Sure you do! After all, you'll never be younger than you are right now.

The first thing to do is put on a pair of cargo pants. These pants have more pockets than you'll know what to do with. Put in a map, passport, alarm clock, flashlight, rape whistle, camp stove, money clip, motion sickness pills, sunglasses, iPod, propane curling iron, insect repellant, several pairs of socks, padlock, camera, address book, and Leatherman, and you'll still have seventeen empty pockets to go. Try to balance the weight and bulk evenly up and down your legs, and from front to back. And make sure you can sit and climb stairs without grimacing or requiring the assistance of a stranger.

Next, mix up this Bloody Mary, pour it into a flask, and put it in one of the empty pockets. I know what you're thinking. Tomato juice and Scotch??? I was skeptical too. But nothing else achieves that gritty, train-station-bathroom-y, I've-worn-the-same-clothes-for-a-week flavor quite like this combination. It needs the grated onion too, not just onion powder, to give it pungency and texture, and to help repel thieves. For its size, it's heavy on the Tabasco sauce, but that's good for killing unwelcome intestinal flora. The rosemary leaves, resting on top, tease your nose into thinking you're moseying through the moors. And it's nice and compact, which is critical for traveling light.

If you don't have an actual backpack, you can shove some clothes into a yoga bag, diaper bag, or oversized tote, and head out the door. Now, where should you go? It's fun to take a city bus to a part of town you don't normally visit, and do a little exploring there. Or you could sit in a cafe and listen to rosy-cheeked, dreadlocked college kids talk about their past or present nomadic odysseys. When they ask about what you're up to (and they will), tell them you're in training for a trip there yourself. Pass your flask around, to their delight.

Eventually, you'll feel like it's time to go home. I know I do, no matter how exhilarating the outing has been. The cozy life I've worked hard to build for myself is waiting there. My husband, whom I wouldn't trade for any sojourn in the world, is glad to see me. I've had my belated journey but without the expense, crime, or food poisoning of a real pilgrimage. This Bloody Mary is a perfect way to satisfy the occasional bout of wanderlust, don't you agree? Let it take your mouth to places that your feet secretly yearn to go.

We Should Go to Hawaii More Often

Serves 1

2 shots coconut rum
6 oz. tomato juice, chilled
1 tsp. chopped ginger
1 tsp. chopped Thai basil
1 tsp. curry powder
1 dash fresh lemon juice
Salt and black pepper, to taste
Pickled garlic, to serve

Mix the rum and tomato juice in a Collins glass with crushed ice. Add the ginger, basil, curry powder, and lemon. Stir well, and adjust the flavor with salt and pepper as needed. Serve with pickled garlic, but use it sparingly—or at least, if you find yourself upwind, try not to breathe on anybody.

Suburbanites gone wild!

The two worst things about travel are the TSA and coming back home. You know how it works. Just when you get comfortable with no alarm clocks, no pantyhose, and no housework, the week is up and you have to go back to reality. It always takes me a couple of days to shake off my stress and get into the swing of things. Once I do, (I'll be honest) I could stay in vacation mode a shockingly long time. But alas, duty always calls. If only there were a way to keep the vibe going back on home turf...

When I was nine, my parents took my sister and me to a terrific beach resort. After the trip ended, I thought I'd try prolonging the magic by painting my bedroom ceiling blue and putting a few inches of sand on the floor. Needless to say, my folks and I didn't see eye to eye on that one. However, I continued to wear my bathing suit under my clothes until my sister pronounced me a weirdo and told everyone at school.

At fifteen, I spent an unforgettable week in Mexico with my family. It was on that trip that I learned to drive recklessly, enjoy margaritas, flirt, and tan with baby oil. I had a blast, and although I wanted that week to go on forever, the sensible part of me detected certain peril if I brought those skills home. I put them on hold until I was seventeen, but it just wasn't the same. I did become very popular, though.

My husband and I went to Hawaii on our honeymoon. It was perfect. Starry nights in a hammock, breathtaking sunsets, romantic strolls on the beach... Okay, granted, it was our honeymoon, but for many reasons, it stands out as one of our favorite vacations together. It's fun to rekindle those memories of being sunburned, lazy, worn out from water sports and "other" honeymoon activities. We do this by taking a romantic stroll as often as we can, even if it's in our neighborhood, and many a starry night has seen us snogging in our backyard hammock. But every so often we need a booster shot to our wedded mojo. That's when we put on some ukelele music, haul out the photos, and sit down with a couple of these tropical Bloody Marys.

Regardless of how long it's been since you were there, this is a nifty and inexpensive way to transport you back to the islands, *wikiwiki*. For one thing, you can hardly order a drink in the South Pacific and not encounter rum, coconut, and ginger. But since we're talking Bloody Marys here and not daiquiris, it's got to have some savory balance. Thai basil sharpens the rum's sweetness just enough to marry it to the tomato juice. Lemon helps keep it from running too far to the sweet side. But it's the curry powder that really kicks it in the *holoholo*. It powers up the exotic deliciousness of the coconut essence and vice versa. A little pickled garlic, a paper umbrella, a grass skirt, and you're on your way. This irresistible Bloody Mary is truly *no ka 'oi* ("the best," for all you *malihinis*).

Don't keep this smug reverie all to yourself. Buy a few silk leis and invite the gang over to enjoy your vacation snapshots, no matter how vintage. Only your real friends will accept the invitation, but even so, I have to warn you: it's not the photos they're interested in. They'll come for the *pupus*, but they'll stay for the Bloody Marys.

What a Perfect Day for a Picnic

Serves 2

12 oz. canned tomato juice
1 tsp. each of black pepper, lemon pepper, celery salt,
   chili-garlic sauce, Worcestershire sauce, and grated
   horseradish
1 tsp. lemon juice
2 jiggers vodka
4 green olives, to serve

Shake the tomato juice, seasonings, and lemon juice well in a mason jar (if you're staying home, you can whisk everything together in a glass pitcher). Fill two 12-ounce plastic cups with ice cubes, add 1 jigger of vodka to each, and top off both cups with the Bloody Mary mix. Float two olives on top of each drink. Yogi Bear would sell Boo Boo to a Third World sweatshop for what's in this picnic basket.

Be careful! The only thing I want on the rocks is my Bloody Mary!

Dining al fresco always looks elegant in French Impressionist paintings and in old Doris Day movies, but it can be such a hassle to pull off. Something as innocuous as a forgotten butter knife can spell disaster. The key is to keep it simple, and prepare enough in advance so you're not stuck scrambling around for fluffy toothpicks or Sterno at the last minute. I've compiled a list of FAQs to help guide you through the mysteries of a successful outdoor feast.

* *How do I decide what food to bring?* A lot depends on the weather. If the temperature is in the nineties or above, it's best to minimize foods that contain mayonnaise or dairy products. You want your picnic to be a memorable occasion, but not because of the EMTs that had to pump your stomach. Potato

or rice salads dressed with olive oil are safe to leave out for a little while, and they taste wonderful. Don't get me wrong: cheeses, meats, and even cooked fish are fine to bring along, but only if you have a way to keep them at forty degrees or colder for the duration of your outing. Prepare what you can ahead of time so you won't have to fuss with gadgets or ingredients. A good rule of thumb is to take everything you need, and one or two things you want.

* *I want to sweep my guy off his feet. Any tips?* Cloth napkins, rather than paper, are a nice touch. Same with china plates, stainless steel flatware, and glass drinking vessels. These things add weight to your basket, though, so keep in mind how much you're prepared to carry and how far you may have to hike in order to find a sufficiently secluded spot. It's a definite mood-killer to arrive sweating, out of breath, and clutching your lower spine. Don't forget to pack a soft blanket to spread out on the grass. If all goes according to plan, you'll both want to get horizontal after the meal.

* *What should I wear?* Consider the landscape and any activities you plan to do. You might find yourself tossing a football, playing bocce, dancing in a fountain, or simply listening to live music. In most cases, I'm guessing you will want to leave your Christian Louboutin heels at home. A wrap, cardigan, or jacket is a good idea if you're still picnicking after the sun goes down. A hat can protect you from the harsh midday rays. Speaking of the sun, don't forget sunblock, or for that matter, insect repellant.

* *The whole loaf-of-bread-jug-of-wine-and-thou scene is such a cliché. What are some ingredients for a hip, modern picnic?* I'm glad you asked. You're right, that tired old picnic formula has been done to death. Instead, try a Bloody Mary. It's a sensible choice because, unlike beer or soda pop, it can handle being jostled during transport, and it's not sensitive to being left out in the heat. You can bring it to a brunch as well as to a late-afternoon supper. It's simple to throw together at home and takes up very little room in your cooler. You can even add the vodka ahead of time so there's one less thing to carry. In the cooler, arrange a couple of re-freezable ice packs, a plastic container filled with ice cubes (easier to drain off any water that accumulates), a leak-proof mason jar full of Bloody Mary mix, a vial of vodka (if it's not already in the mason jar), and a Ziploc bag of celery sticks. Remember the mantra: keep it simple, and prep beforehand. Adding ice to a glass and twisting open a jar is about as simple as it gets. And in this case, even the prep is simple—add things to a jar and shake.

Some food pairings to consider are cucumber sandwiches on rye bread, a cold pasta salad, or a quiche with bacon and carmelized onion. The only other things you'll need are napkins, plates, forks, serving utensils, and a couple of glasses. And a blanket to sprawl on.

I hope this has been helpful for planning your pastoral getaway. I'll be looking for you out on a grassy knoll somewhere. You'll be easy to spot; I'll just look for the crowd around your blanket clamoring for your fantastic Bloody Mary recipe.

What's the Guatemalan Phrase for "Please Untie Me"

Serves 3 to 4

1 can tomatillos*
1/4 medium onion
1/2 jalapeño pepper
1 Tbsp. fresh or canned *nopalitos**
Juice of 1/2 lime
1 Tbsp. sugar
1 Tbsp. olive brine
Salt, to taste
Pinch cumin
3–4 shots tequila
3–4 cilantro sprigs, to serve
3–4 cherry tomatoes, to serve
6–8 white cocktail onions, to serve
(* = found in the ethnic food aisle of almost
    any supermarket; *nopalitos* are made from
    the pads of a prickly pear cactus)

Place the tomatillos, onion, jalapeño, nopalitos, lime juice, sugar, olive brine, cumin, and salt in a blender or food processor. Puree until well combined but still chunky rather than smooth. Spoon about 1/2 cup into a cocktail shaker with 1 shot of tequila per drink. Shake well. Serve over ice cubes in poco grande glasses and garnish each with a sprig of cilantro, a cherry tomato, and a couple of cocktail onions.

Um, can I borrow your phone?

N ot for you, the staid air-conditioned tour package. Not for you, the formulaic just-add-water vacation in a box. You wouldn't be caught dead on a cruise or within the confines of a theme park. No, you blithely bought a single ticket to a country you've only heard of, to stay in a city you can't pronounce, to live among people you don't know how to communicate with. Because it's exciting, because you got an unbelievable deal, because you can.

"Then what?" I say.

"Dunno," you say.

"WTF?" I say.

Your plan, if you can call it that, is to hitchhike into town from the airport, where you will walk around until someone offers you lodging. For the next three weeks, you will hang out with the locals and take each day as it comes.

Exciting isn't the word for it. Insane just might cover it, though.

I did a little research, and I'm pretty sure you have no idea what pitfalls await you. Here's just a sampling:

* If you are hiking near cattle, chances are there's a bull nearby. Think large, mean, and in possession of long, sharp horns. Hopefully the bull hasn't seen you yet, and if that's the case, continue to walk slowly and as quietly as possible. Once he spots you, don't scream or try to outrun him. Very slowly take off your shirt. If the bull charges, throw the shirt and run (yes, now you can run) the other way while he is distracted. You will be momentarily safe from the bull, but now you are walking around a foreign country topless.

* Banditos are in the habit of stopping buses and robbing and/or raping the people aboard. Tell me again how much safer you'll be in crowds versus walking around alone. With or without a shirt.

* Don't overlook the smallest bandito of all, the botfly. The larvae crawl under your skin through an opening as small as a mosquito bite. As the larva grows, it causes intense itching at the entry site. As it grows even bigger and moves around, you will experience a high degree of pain. People have tried many different ways of extracting botfly larvae while it's alive. None of them work because the critter is attached to you from the inside with tailhooks. Luckily, there is a YouTube video that tells you how to smother the little bugger and extract it, but you have neither internet access nor a shirt. Make sure to watch that video before you leave home!

* The Guatemalan Travel website proudly states that you are guaranteed 99.7 percent of the time

to have a great time in their country. However, after sifting through page after page of warnings, I found these facts: (1) tourists are advised not to walk, drive, or take a taxi between 6 PM and 6 AM. I guess you're supposed to go to dinner on a mule. (2) There is a special police division whose sole purpose is to keep tourists safe. Hmmm... That 0.3 percent must get in an awful lot of trouble. (3) The police force, tourist or otherwise, has "poor training and equipment, and are not to be expected to solve crimes." They probably don't even have shirts.

Rather than put yourself squarely in harm's way, why not stay on home soil and have a Bloody Mary? It's got everything your vacation's got: alluring Latin flavors, excitement, frugality, and ease of execution (the other kind, thank God). It's not even red, contrary to what you might expect; it's avocado green. The cumin, lime, *nopalitos*, and jalapeño will remind you of the ingredients common in Mexican and South American cooking. The sugar helps to temper the heat and smooth the edges of the tomatillos and tequila. Here, have another. Isn't that the next best thing to being there? You can even take off your shirt if you want.

I Spent Three Months in Palm Desert One Weekend

Serves 6

8 medium tomatoes
1 tsp. Worcestershire sauce
1 tsp. hot pepper sauce
1 Tbsp. horseradish
1/2 cup lemon juice
1/2 tsp. coarse kosher salt
1/4 tsp. ground black pepper
6 Tbsp. aquavit
1/2 cup chopped fresh basil leaves, to serve

Combine the first seven ingredients in a food processor, and blend until smooth. Transfer the mixture to an 11" × 7" × 2" baking dish. Freeze until it starts to set around the edges, stirring occasionally, about 1 hour. Continue to freeze, without stirring, until firm (2 more hours). Remove the pan from the freezer, and let it stand until you can scrape the slush into flakes with a fork, 20 to 30 minutes. Divide the flakes among six martini glasses, pouring a tablespoon of aquavit over each. Garnish with basil leaves and serve.

It's so hot, I might have to take off my shoes and socks!

I f you've been paying attention, you may remember that I'm the girl who's always cold. I embrace any and all opportunities to spend time in warm places. Saunas. Hot tubs. Bikram yoga class. But I have never in all my born days experienced heat like the Mojave Desert in late summer. I arrived one evening, when the temperature was a pleasant eighty-eight degrees. After breakfast the next day, I went out to the car to get my sunglasses, preparing to walk around a bit. The air temperature outside hit me like a cast iron skillet. Grabbing the car door handle raised an ugly blister on two of my fingers. And when I finally got the door open, there were my sunglasses, in a congealed puddle of melted plastic. Needless to say, I then did something I thought I would never do in a million years: I began to search for a place to cool off.

The locals have this all figured out. They'll shrug off the

triple-digit temperatures because "it's a dry heat." Who do they think they're kidding? Many are so-called snowbirds, which means they fly north to more realistic climes during the hot spells. The less fortunate inhabitants survive by having state-of-the-art air conditioners in every possible indoor space, and by not going outside if they can help it. They distract themselves with spa treatments, shopping malls, 5 AM tennis matches, and ice-cold liquor. When scientists finally decide that the earth is no longer fit to sustain human life and they build dwellings on the surface of the sun, the Palm Desert set will feel right at home. They'll be hermetically sealed inside their houses, saying, "Sure is hot today, but lucky for us it's a dry heat."

I couldn't stand the heat, so I got into the kitchen. I managed to get through the weekend thanks to this refreshing frozen Bloody Mary recipe. Whether you're planning to travel to a scorching locale, bracing for a heat wave on your home turf, or simply battling your own "personal summers," you're going to love these little caraway-flavored treats. They're like savory snow cones for grown-ups. This recipe makes enough for a small brunch crowd, but you could also keep the mixture in a covered tub in the freezer and scoop some out whenever you like.

You'll notice that there is some prep work to be done early on, and the rest of the time is spent waiting for the mixture to freeze. It's best to start the process early so the hard part is over with by the time the temperature soars. Let's assume you've got all the ingredients at hand. The blending part will only take you ten minutes or so. Don't go too far away for the next hour, because you'll have to stir the slush occasionally. (I looked up "occasionally" in a cooking terms book, and it said "once in a while." Then I researched how long a "while" is, and it is defined as "somewhere between a few hours and a few months." Not helpful.) Wondering what to do with yourself for the following two hours? Here are some ideas:

If you are preparing to host a brunch, you'll need this time to get ready. A simple frittata, a fruit salad, some store-bought scones, and you're done.

If it's just you, you could:

1. Put together skimpy outfits on www.polyvore. com.

2. Familiarize yourself with the signs of heatstroke and what to do about it.

3. Splash around in the pool, if you have one; a cool bath, if you don't.

4. Call all your friends and ask, "Hot enough for ya?"

See if you really can fry an egg on the sidewalk, the hood of your car, the patio furniture, etc.

Okay, now you can take the pan out of the freezer to let it soften. Use this time to clean up the egg messes outside. In under thirty minutes, you're good to go! *Ahhh.* Maybe this dry heat will prove to be tolerable after all.

GARNISH

Location, Location, Location

I've always found that the most soothing way to refresh myself after a red-eye is with my favorite red drink. The next time you travel, you will no doubt want to sample the local Bloody Mary creations at journey's end. A word of caution: as a wide-eyed little girl named Dorothy once remarked, "I don't think we're in Kansas anymore." You may be surprised to see what shows up on your table.

* In the southern United States, you'll find decent Bloody Marys but no vegetation to speak of. (They like to go light on the garnish.) However, they pride themselves on premium vodka, so as not to disappoint.

* In Minnesota, a Bloody Mary is commonly served with a beer on the side.

* Brits know that "Bloody Mary" is Cockney rhyming slang for "hairy." (You don't want to know what appears on the table.)

* Ready for a real adventure? In the night market of Taipei, a Bloody Mary is made with turtle blood and whiskey.

PART VI

Transformations

Take some tomato juice, a celery stick, and a fistful of pepper. After mixing, sniff, discard, then proceed, volcano-nosed to an old hotel where you will fit in among the gin-blossom snouts who frequent these establishments. You should then order a properly prepared Bloody Mary (known only to trusty barkeeps) amid the appropriate décor.
—Chris Lindland, entrepreneur, trendsetter, comedy writer, modern-day Midas

If Madonna didn't reinvent herself every few years, she'd still be prancing around in pointy bras and torn fishnets. Be honest with yourself. Are you due for a makeover? When was the last time you changed your hair? Reordered your priorities? Feathered your nest? These five recipes start with thoughtful introspection and end with a fresh outlook on life. They're made of sterner stuff than the preceding Bloody Marys, and a few of them will require a certain amount of resolve to put together. But like any transformation that's worth doing, it's worth doing it right.

We Need a Bigger Garage

Serves 1

    1 jigger vodka
    3 oz. Bloody Mary mix
    3 oz. canned condensed beef bouillon
    Black pepper and hot sauce, to taste
        (I like about 1/2 tsp. each.)
    1 green onion, to serve

Pour the vodka, Bloody Mary mix, and bouillon over crushed or cubed ice in a highball glass and stir. Add the pepper and hot sauce as desired, and garnish with the green onion.

Honey? Did you say we have too many trucks or ducks?

I dedicate this Bloody Mary to everyone who has come to the realization that they just have too much stuff.

When did humans become enslaved as Keepers of Stuff? Neanderthal man and his wife were primarily concerned with survival. If one clan or another seemed to be surviving particularly well, people would saunter by and look inside their cave to see what the secret to their success was. Often, the clan had more bear fur or arrowheads or something than the others, so it became clear even to primitive man that more stuff = better life.

Egyptians used to entomb their dead pharoahs with all of their stuff. That way, if they found the need to take a boat ride or change clothes in the afterlife, everything would be at their fingertips. This taught the Egyptians that more stuff = better afterlife.

After the Depression, nobody had much stuff. It was easy to see who was hardest hit, economically speaking, because they had less or worse-quality stuff than their neighbors. Twentieth-century Americans knew that more stuff = better livelihood.

Today, thanks to marketing geniuses like my husband, people buy more stuff than they need. They live among it, to varying degrees, but a lot of it gets toted off to Mini Storage or, if they're lucky enough to have one, the garage. Tom and I are guilty of it ourselves. In fact, we have both a garage *and* a storage unit. That's because we each had a lot of stuff, then we got married and combined our stuff, and then my parents moved to a care facility and gave us their stuff. I sometimes think, if our house caught on fire, and we had mere seconds to get out but could take anything we wanted, what would it be? Certainly nothing in the garage.

Once a year or so, it's a good idea to cast an unsentimental eye around the garage and get rid of junk that's taking up valuable space. When we do, we like to have a Bloody Mary first. This one gets us in the spring cleaning mood like no other. One reason is that it's made from things that we always have on hand—vodka, bottled Bloody Mary mix, beef bouillon, and black pepper. No need to run to the store for special stuff. Two, there's not an extraneous or redundant flavor on the list. A place for everything, and everything in its place. Three, because it tastes meaty and serious, it seems fitting to drink one on Garage Day. Even if your garage is full of pink tutus, you still want to approach stuff management with grim seriousness. Four, I don't know about you, but vodka is one of the few things that gives me the courage to go out there and face that four-walled landfill I used to park my car in.

Organizing specialists often recommend going through your stuff with the help of an impartial friend. He or she doesn't have any sentimentality attached to the stuff, unless the chocolate fountain on the give-away pile was a gift from said friend. If that happens, angrily (but clearly) mutter something about how your kid/dog/mother-in-law is always messing with your stuff, and go back in the house for another round of Bloody Marys pronto. You can tackle your stuff another day (and with another friend).

All I Need Is Comfort Food and a Little "Me" Time

Serves 1

3 oz. extra spicy Bloody Mary mix
I jigger vodka
I oz. plain yogurt
I tsp. grated onion
I tsp. freshly ground black pepper
I parsley sprig

Place all the ingredients (except the parsley) in a cocktail shaker filled with ice cubes, and shake until well blended. Pour over fresh ice in an Old Fashioned glass and garnish with the parsley sprig.

Flooded with youthful resilience (and Prozac),
Katherine finds her happy place.

What a week! The deadlines, the meetings, the traffic—oh my! It's a wonder you can even think straight. Thank goodness for Saturday, the Gregorian calendar's gift to you. It's one of only four or five sacred days per month for you to recharge your body and soul. The word Saturday comes from an obscure Ukrainian phrase, meaning "to be your own best friend." This disabuses the previously held notion that Saturday meant "day of laundry, cleaning the gutters, and balancing the checkbook."

In honor of that Eastern European philosophy, I'm going to teach you an ancient Saturday ritual that's guaranteed to titivate and inspire you.

> ✱ **Friday night:** (1) Take a few minutes to tidy up your boudoir. Pick up the magazines, hang up your clothes, take dirty dishes to the kitchen, and

change the sheets. When you open your eyes tomorrow morning, you want everything to be as
pleasant as possible. Remember, you are a jewel,
and you deserve a beautiful setting. (2) Disable
your alarm clock. (3) Put on something decadent
but comfortable to sleep in. No sweatpants or
flannel allowed! Think silky boxers, a lacy cami,
a soft, lightweight cardigan.

* **Saturday:** (1) Sleep as late as you want or as late
as possible. If you've got roommates, children, or
pets, heaven help you; do the best you can. (2) By
all means, take care of any physical needs that
arise, yours and/or your bedmate's. (3) Take five
or six really deep, cleansing breaths, preferably in
front of an open window. It does amazing things
for your mood. (4) Send aforementioned bedmate
to get the newspaper and fry up some bacon. If it's
just you, get up and do it yourself; it's worth the
sacrifice. And while you're up, mix yourself this
Russian-inspired Bloody Mary. Bring everything
back to bed with you. (5) It's very important to
linger in this position for a long, long time; really
savor every detail. The mouthwatering aroma of
bacon. The sound of birdsong outside. The lurid
headlines. The whisper of your silk unmention-
ables. The creamy astringency of the Bloody
Mary. The daylight casting soft shadows on your
comforter. Before you can say *"Szeretem!"* ("I
love it!"), you're on your way to improved mental
health.

There is, however, a certain protocol that must be followed if
the ritual is to have optimum results. It comes from hundreds of

years of Eastern European tradition, and is specific to the Bloody Mary portion of Operation Recharge.

* When you have alcohol, it must be drunk until it is gone.

* One should not put a glass with alcohol back on the table.

* One should not make a long interruption between the first and second glasses.

* It is not allowed to pour out a bottle's contents while holding it from the bottom.

* It is not allowed to fill a glass being held in the air.

This may be your only day to pamper yourself for quite a while, so take the time to do it by the book. You won't regret it.

Good Help Is So Hard to Find

Serves 4

The tomato water:
  3½ lbs. very ripe tomatoes, quartered
  2 chopped jalapeño peppers
  1/4 red onion, diced
  Small pinch sugar
  Large pinch salt
  1/2 lime
  1/2 lemon
  1/2 orange
  30" × 36" piece of cheesecloth

The Bloody Mary mix:
  Himalayan pink salt
  16 oz. homemade tomato water
  8 oz. citrus vodka
  Several basil leaves, slivered, to serve
  8 cherry tomatoes, to serve

To make the tomato water, puree the first five ingredients in a food processor. Line a large colander with the cheesecloth and place on top of a larger glass bowl. Pour the puree into the colander and allow it to seep through the cheesecloth into the bowl. Cover both the colander and the bowl with plastic wrap (with the colander still sitting in the bowl), and refrigerate 12 to 24 hours. By then, the bowl will contain clear liquid and all the tomato pulp will still be in the colander. Pull the sides of the cheesecloth up over the puree to form a large ball and press out any last bits of water. Don't squeeze too hard or the tomato water will be cloudy or take on a reddish tinge. Remove the colander from the bowl, and store the pulp for future use in sauces or soup. Hold a clean colander over the bowl and squeeze in the juice from the lime, lemon, and orange. Store in the refrigerator for up to seven days in an airtight container, or use immediately.

When you're ready to get crackin', rim four Old Fashioned glasses with the Himalayan salt, and fill each with ice cubes. In a separate glass, combine 4 ounces tomato water and 2 ounces vodka, and stir. Transfer into one of the serving glasses. Repeat for the remaining servings. Add slivers of basil and two halved cherry tomatoes as a garnish. It's rather fun to putter around in the kitchen, isn't it? Perhaps you should give the servants a day off more often.

Ah, here's the young lady from the temp agency now.

I've often said that if you want something done right, you've got to do it yourself. But with the increasing demands of raising children, keeping a clean and smooth-running household, maintaining the landscaping, holding down a job, being a supportive life partner, staying in shape, and participating in the community, it's hard to do it right let alone do it at all. Thank goodness there are things like Facebook, Twitter, Plaxo, LinkedIn, and Four Square to keep you abreast of what your friends are up to. Through the magic of the internet, you can catch the news, gossip, entertainment, and weather anytime of the day or night. And you have instant coffee, a hands-free cell headset, and a self-cleaning oven, but you're still falling behind.

You clearly need a virtual assistant. Or Mr. French. Or an Office Betty. Or a wife. But you'll settle for a Gal Friday for the time being.

Action Item #1: Post a job description. "Busy Renaissance woman seeks personal assistant for light office, childcare, and household duties. Shrinking violets need not apply." Celebrate your clear-headed resolve with a pristine, clear Bloody Mary. As a matter of fact, make a big enough batch of tomato water to see you through this tumultuous week. Speaking of the faint at heart, this recipe is no walk in the park! It takes skill and patience to do it right, but the results will be well worth it. You will end up with four of the most unusual, elegant Bloodies you've ever seen. Your high standards and keen sense of aesthetics demand the best, and this recipe delivers on its promise to give you just that.

Action Item #2: Respond to the most promising applicants and set up interviews for the next few days. Reward the clear-eyed way you culled the best resumes from the stack with another Bloody Mary. You're never too busy to notice how the pink salt rim reminds you of a necklace Princess Diana used to wear. Now there was a woman who knew how to delegate.

Action Item #3: On Interview Day, be friendly but clear about what your expectations are. Don't show bias against any applicant, no matter how appalling or unsuitable they seem. At the end of the day, review your notes carefully so everyone you spoke to will stay clear in your mind. Help yourself to another clear Bloody Mary as you ponder the possibilities:

* Applicant A wouldn't stop pacing and looking furtively out the window every few minutes, and the only identification in her wallet was her bus pass and a folded copy of her GED. When you asked her if she had ever worked using another name, she pointed out her prison tats and said she used to be known as Dirtbox Demon.

* Applicant B came in wearing Birkenstocks and white tube socks. The name on her driver's license

and resume said Agnes Morton, but she asked you to call her "Sunshower." Before she left, she said you could get rid of that stick up your ass if your office had better Feng Shui.

* Applicant C wanted to know if she could have an expense account at Starbucks or at least a company car. She told you she could type eighty-five words per minute but only with her thumbs. She ate all the mints out of the bowl on your desk and then made herself throw up.

* Applicant D had a large metal ring through the middle of her face and smelled so bad you had to put her chair outside after she left. She spent the interview rolling her own cigarettes. When you asked her about her Megadeth tattoo, she made a disconcerting and rather obscene gesture in your direction.

   Sounds like Bloody Mary time to me. *Clearly.* Heavy on the vodka this time. It won't change the look or consistency of the drink one whit.

Action Item #4: Shred all applications. Get a book on Feng Shui and another on multitasking. Propose a toast to you and your newfound clarity with another Bloody Mary. While we're on the subject, that certainly was a magnificent crafting of a tricky cocktail. But after all is said and done, if you want something done right, do it yourself. That much is crystal clear.

Blondes May Have More Fun,
But Brunettes Have Better Fun

Makes about 1 quart (4–5 servings)

The Bloody Mary mix:
  32 oz. tomato juice
  1 Tbsp. horseradish
  1 Tbsp. lime juice
  1 Tbsp. lemon juice
  1 tsp. onion powder
  1 tsp. garlic powder
  1/2 tsp. cracked black pepper
  1 tsp. Old Bay seasoning
  1 dash Tabasco sauce
  1 dash Worcestershire sauce

The infused vodka:
  1 large Roma tomato
  Olive oil
  Garlic powder, sea salt, and freshly ground
    black pepper, to taste
  16 oz. Skyy vodka
  1 handful fresh rosemary leaves
  Sea salt, to serve
  1/4 cup kalamata olives (plus 2 olives per serving,
    to garnish)
  4–5 lime wedges, to serve

To make the Bloody Mary mix, combine all the ingredients together in a half-gallon container, and refrigerate (it will keep for up to 2 weeks).

To make the infused vodka, slice a ripe Roma tomato into 8 slices. Brush the slices with olive oil and dust liberally with the garlic powder, sea salt, and black pepper. Place the slices on a cookie sheet and bake in a 200-degree oven for 4 to 5 hours. Remove the pan from the oven when the tomato slices look shriveled but not browned. Put the vodka, rosemary, 1/2 cup of olives, and tomato slices in a quart mason jar with a tight-fitting lid, and marinate for 2 days in the refrigerator (though it will keep indefinitely if you wish to use it later).

To serve, combine 2 parts vodka with 1 part Bloody Mary mix in a large pitcher. While still chilled, pour straight up in martini glasses with a sea salt rim. Garnish each serving with 2 olives and a lime wedge. (Are we having fun yet?)

*Boys wouldn't look twice at me
when I was a blonde. Now my
phone rings nonstop!*

I, too, crossed over to the Dark Side. And I've been hitting the bottle ever since.

I'd been working as an actress for about seven years when I signed with a different agency. My gung-ho new booking agents were determined to break me into the modeling world as well. Upon first laying eyes on me in person, Kit and Nina declared, "But first, you need a hair 9-1-1!" Before I could ask what that meant, I was deposited into a swivel chair, draped in black nylon, and promised I would emerge looking "like a woman who would drive a Lexus." Mendy, my hairdresser from that day forward, proceeded to trim nearly twelve inches worth of my two-hundred-dollar blond highlights, then colored what was left a deep espresso brown. It changed my life. Not only did it open the door to more and better modeling jobs, but I became more confident. My voice got richer. My posture straightened. I swear, even my breath got better! People who had previously paid no attention to me were asking for my business card. Suddenly it made total sense why Archie drooled over Veronica all those years while poor, sweet Betty waited in the wings.

Lots of modern celebrities have ditched their pale locks and hopped on the brunette bandwagon, too. Reese Witherspoon, Mary Kate Olsen, Ashlee Simpson, Scarlett Johansson, Kate Hudson, Britney Spears, Lindsay Lohan, and Cameron Diaz, to name a few. Nicole Richie commented via Twitter following her transition: "I went brunette. I feel smarter already." To quote Mike Doughty, "All them tremendous brunettes around!" Why the change, do you suppose? If I had to guess, and I do, the young ladies on the list are fairly young and might have needed a boost in the direction of Take Me Seriously (something even Marilyn Monroe would probably vouch for). They've satisfied the urgings of their wild hairs, and are now ready to grow up and put down some roots (sorry, puns are like split ends for me...just when I think they're all under control, here comes another one).

According to Elena Gorgon, a life and style editor, gentlemen really don't prefer blondes anymore. Here are a few reasons why.

* Dark-haired women are more likely to earn an annual salary over $65,000 as compared to blondes and redheads in identical occupations.

* Seventy-five percent of men and women believe brunettes are smarter than blondes, and 71 percent would choose a brunette life partner, all else being equal. Dark-haired women have the reputation of being less moody, more genuine, and more intelligent than their blonde counterparts.

* Brunettes are more confident and assertive. They rate themselves above average in bed.

* A survey of men revealed that the majority feel more successful with a brunette on their arm.

So I pose a question to you: are we having fun yet?

More Fun	Better Fun
Baby-doll tops	A slit-to-the-waist Chanel gown
Beer bongs	Bloody Marys
Wii golf	Capoeira
Fort Lauderdale	Mykonos, Greece
The Bachelor	My Netflix Watch Instantly queue
Karaoke	Opera (go to www. barihunks.com to see why)

Now you're getting the picture. Vodka is fun, but vodka infused with rosemary and kalamata olives is *better* fun. Classic Bloody Marys are fun, but this smoky, zesty version is better fun. Old Bay seasoning and onion powder lift it head and shoulders above the mundane. Drive your Lexus to the store and pick up some Clairol Nice 'N Easy in Darkest Brown, and any of the Bloody Mary ingredients you might be missing. Start the vodka marinating, and then color your hair. Next, plan a party to unveil your new look/persona. This recipe makes about five servings, so no need to scrimp on the guest list. On party day, stir together the tomato mixture in a half-gallon container. Put out some lovely hors d'oeuvres. All set? Great! Open the door and get ready for the compliments. I'm not sure who will receive more, you or your partner in crime, Bloody Mary.

I Need a Hobby Now That the Kids Have Left Home

Serves about 25

- 1 Roma tomato
- 1 brandywine tomato
- 1 green jalapeño pepper
- 1 red jalapeño pepper
- 3 banana peppers
- 1 dill pickle
- 2–3 fresh garlic cloves
- 2–3 green olives
- Pinch celery salt
- Pinch lemon pepper seasoning
- 1 heaping Tbsp. each of creamy horseradish, barbecue sauce, mesquite marinade, yellow mustard, and horseradish pub mustard
- 1/4 cup each of lemon juice and lime juice
- 2 46-oz. cans vegetable juice
- 2 Tbsp. freshly ground peppercorn blend, or to taste
- 1 750-ml. bottle Hangar One Chipotle Vodka
- 4 limes, cut into wedges, to serve
- A large handful of edible flowers from apple blossoms, hyacinth, roses, marigolds, carnations, or primroses, (enough for 1–2 per drink), to serve (optional)

Wash the tomatoes. Score the bottom skin in a cross.

Simmer the tomatoes in a pot of water to loosen the skin. Once it begins to peel, remove them from the water and peel off their skin.

Chop up the skinless tomatoes and remove some of the hard white meat if there is any. Then put in a blender and set aside.

Wash and trim the green and red jalapeños, slicing off the bottoms, stems, and the seed sacs. Dice into a few pieces and add to the blender.

Take the banana peppers and remove the stems; add to the blender.

Cut off the stem of the dill pickle, if there is one, then slice the pickle into a couple pieces and add it to the blender.

Squeeze the garlic cloves through a garlic press and into the blender.

Add the celery salt, lemon pepper, horseradish, barbecue sauce, mesquite marinade, yellow mustard, and horseradish mustard to the blender, and liquefy everything that's in the blender up to this point.

At this time, the spices, or what I like to call "the essence" of the Bloody Mary, should be a thick, creamy substance. Pour it off into a 1-quart mason jar or similar container. Then rinse the blender with the lemon and lime juice, getting out as much as you can and pouring it all off into the jar. Shake up the jar a bit to make sure the juices get into the mix.

Let the Bloody Mary essence stew in the refrigerator for 1 to 2 days.

Add the Bloody Mary essence to a larger juice or gallon container. Pour in the cans of vegetable juice, using some to rinse out the smaller container that held the essence. Add the peppercorn blend.

Shake well until everything is mixed properly. At this point you want to let the whole thing set for a day or so, so that the flavors start to meld. Then you should be good to go. I recommend tasting at this point and tweaking the amounts of salt, lemon and lime juice as needed. And because Bloody Marys, like patience, are their own reward.

To make each serving, fill a cocktail shaker with ice and add 1 part vodka to 3 parts mix. Then shake it 'til you make it! Strain over fresh ice cubes in a highball glass, add a straw, and perch a lime wedge on the edge of the glass. For the big finish, throw in a couple choice blossoms from your bountiful garden—a real feast for the senses.

Mary, Mary, in millinery,
how does your garden grow?

I didn't see this empty nest thing coming. I thought it would be, well, maybe not fun exactly, but peaceful. Relaxing. Like the end of yoga class when you get to just lie on your back and breathe. After all, the kids had been out of the house for summer camp, outdoor school, and band trips, a week here and a week there, and it was great. It meant less cooking, laundry, picking up clutter, driving here and there, pestering about chores, homework, curfew, yadda yadda. I had time to catch up on projects and, yes, relax a bit. But I neglected to realize two key facts: I forgot that my son and daughter had never left home for very long, and never both at the same time. I cried every day of the younger one's freshman year. Right before they were both due home for the summer, I was determined to pull myself together, and find something to occupy my hands and my mind. Gardening seemed to fit the bill. If you're an empty nester like me, maybe you should give it a try too.

There are lots of perks to growing your own food. One, you know where it's been. Two, it allows you to lavish your nurturing talents on something that doesn't talk back or want to borrow the car. Three, given the cost of a college education, it's either eat out of your own backyard or the dumpster behind Trader Joe's. The downside is that it keeps you busy only from spring (planning, tilling) to fall (harvest time). For that reason, I planted a Bloody Mary garden. Not only is the growing of the ingredients labor intensive, but crafting the drink itself (twelve steps!) is enough to keep your mind off your troubles. And if you learn how to can your spanking fresh, organic, watered-with-a-mother's-tears pro-duce, you can enjoy homegrown Bloody Marys all winter long.

This garden will require surprisingly little space. All you need is a sunny spot about the size of a dining room table. Go to the nursery and pick up the specified tomato, jalapeño, garlic, and ba-nana pepper plants. If you really want to be busy, pick up lemon and lime trees as well, and a cucumber plant to make the pickles. Arrange the plantings so that everything has enough room to get adequate sunlight, and spread out as needed. A fantastic resource for decoding terms like "mulching," "compost," and "deadhead-ing" is a book by my friend Jean Ann VanKrevelen called *Grocery Gardening*. Her passion is infectious, and she can walk you through the whole process without making you feel intimidated.

Look, I managed to survive my kids leaving home, and so will you. Think of it as time for yourself that you've earned, like a sabbatical. So go out and plunge your hands into the dewy soil. Listen to the birds' conversations. Soak up some vitamin D. Marvel at each blossom that will soon become a succulent treat. And here's something else to consider: kids always come back, sooner or later. And when they do, hand them a Bloody Mary that took you six months to make. They'll be impressed.

GARNISH

The Bartender's Friend: A Glossary

Use this chart to challenge your friends to a game of Stump the Bartender.

Cool Name	Doesn't Have	Has Instead
Bloody Maria	vodka	tequila
Danish Mary	vodka	aquavit
Bully Mary, Bloody Bull	plain tomato juice	half tomato juice, half beef broth
Highland Mary	vodka	blended Scotch
Cuban Mary	vodka	light rum
Red Snapper, London Mary	vodka	gin
Michelada	vodka	Mexican beer
Bloody Geisha, Bloody Maru	vodka	sake
Brown Mary, Whiskey Mary, Bloody Molly	vodka	whiskey
Bloody Bishop	just vodka	sherry and vodka
Bull Shot, Bloody Caesar, Seaside Mary	tomato juice	beef broth
Clammy Mary	tomato juice	Clamato
Bloody 8, 8 Ball	tomato juice	V8
Russian Mary	nothing omitted	plain yogurt
Bloody Mariner	tomato juice	clam juice
Bloody Pearl Harbor	just vodka	vodka and rum
Bluegrass Mary	vodka	bourbon
Italian Bloody Mary	vodka	grappa
Virgin Mary, Bloody Shame	alcohol	nothing
Bloody Fairy	vodka	absinthe
Bloody Pirate	vodka	dark rum
Red Eye	vodka	beer
Bloody Maureen	vodka	Guinness

PART VII

Commiserations

Oh Bloody Mary.
You bring sunshine to my day,
When I need you most.
   —An original haiku by Judy Bennett, August 28, 2007
      (1 hour after making my daughter's first $52,000 tuition
      payment)

As any country song will tell you, a good stiff drink can help take the edge off a heartache. And heartaches, like Bloody Marys, come in lots of flavors. There's frustration, boredom, despair, disappointment, and plain old woe-is-me. The best remedy for each is antidotal. If you lack sunshine, have a big bright glass of vitamin C. If you got kicked when you're down, put something cold on your wounds. If you're broke, have a cheap but nourishing meal. Bad news to deliver? A searing cup of courage will do the trick. You get the idea. Let Bloody Mary help you put the "party" in your pity party.

It's Not You, It's Me

Serves 1

3–4 cherry tomatoes
2 lime wedges
Pinch of salt
1–2 tsp. Bloody Mary seasoning
   (Demitri's or Angostura does a nice job)
2–4 fresh basil leaves
3 oz. tomato juice
1 jigger cucumber-flavored vodka

Muddle the cherry tomatoes and lime wedges in a cocktail shaker. Add the salt, seasoning blend, basil (minus enough to garnish), tomato juice, vodka, and some ice cubes. Shake well and serve in an Old Fashioned glass garnished with the remaining basil leaves. Now there's a match made in heaven.

When Hal told Tina that they should date other people, she didn't think he meant right NOW!

The bell curve of relationships goes something like this: Two people meet. They find things in common. They sample each other's interests so they have even more in common. Their friends, hobbies, toiletries, and body parts become intertwined. One person changes his or her mind and makes a mental shift to disengage. Person Two senses the shift and works all the harder to be "perfect" and therefore indispensable. Person One does something heinous to create some space between them. Person Two gets the message and an awkward silence ensues. Often there is retaliation, drunk dialing, and/or rumor-spreading during this phase. Mutual friends begin to take sides. Eventually, both parties pick up their toiletries and other baggage from the relationship and part ways. Of course, this is how the majority of relationships go, but a sane person doesn't go around marrying everyone they fall for (hear that, Zsa Zsa?). And if they do, that only postpones the inevitable. Also, don't believe it when someone tells you their breakup occurred as the result of a mutual agreement. "Oh, Susan and I just grew apart." Really? What are the odds that humans get sick of each other at *exactly the same time*? What that statement actually means is "Susan turned into a total bitch when I cashed out our IRA to have transgender surgery."

Breakups are always uncomfortable, no matter if you're the breaker or the breakee. The key to surviving one is trying to remember who you are as an individual, not as half of a couple. Learning to say "I" and not "we." Owning your feelings, rather than assigning blame. *Oof.* This is getting pretty heavy, even for me. Let me put it in a context you can wrap your taste buds, er, head, around.

Bloody Marys are full of distinctive, great-tasting ingredients (qualities) in proportions that work in harmony with each other. Like this one, for instance: cherry tomatoes and limes are wonderful on their own, and twice as wonderful together. Rather than puree themselves into an indistinguishable, romantic froth, they've maintained their basic natures while allowing their fluids to mingle. Their friends—Spices, Tomato Juice, Basil, and Vodka—surround them, support them, but don't define them. Then comes the day when Lime, for whatever reason, tries to drive a wedge between the happy pair. How does Ms. Tomato respond? I'll tell you how. She does not try to cower behind Tomato Juice or run off with the exotic Spices, because she never lost her identity in the relationship. She remains strong and respects Lime's right to do the same. Lime, meanwhile, realizes the futility in trying to overpower her and takes his place as her equal. So, in the end, even though their relationship is all muddled up, they can still play off each other's strengths and come out better than the sum of their parts. This is a script for how relationships ought to go; I take it yours looked more like Jamba Juice. Poor baby. You know what they say: when at first you get pureed, try, try again.

Now that you've got the Bloody Mary and your breakup survival strategy figured out, how about a play list for some self-righteous booty- and cocktail-shakin'?

"These Boots Were Made for Walkin',"
   by Nancy Sinatra
"Since U Been Gone," by Kelly Clarkson
"Smile," by Lily Allen
"Would I Lie to You?" by Annie Lennox
"It's Not Right (Remix)," by Whitney
   Houston
"Ex-Girlfriend," by No Doubt
"I Will Survive," by Gloria Gaynor
"Here I Go Again," by Whitesnake
"Goodbye to You," by Scandal
"Time for Me to Fly," by REO Speedwagon
"Someday," by Mariah Carey
"Respect," by Aretha Franklin

Any way you slice it, breaking up a love affair is no fun. But life goes on. Next time, remember to keep the muddling in the cocktail shaker and not in your heart, and you'll come out just fine.

I Can't Manage My Money If I Don't Have Any

Serves 1

- 1 beef ramen seasoning packet
- 1 oz. tomato juice or V8
- 1 ½ oz. vodka
- 1 packet Taco Bell hot sauce

In any small glass, dissolve the seasoning packet in the tomato juice. Add the vodka and hot sauce to taste, stir well, and take as a shot. Talk about an economic stimulus package!

*Whatever you're selling,
I'll take two.*

Remember when shopping used to be fun? When a little re-
tail therapy could counteract even the worst of days? Did
we appreciate the power we held in our hands—that anything
in the world could be ours with just a swipe of a card? I know I
didn't, until that sickening day when the salesgirl at Nordstrom
gave me an apologetic smile (lips coated in the very latest MAC
Viva Glam VI, just to spite me, I'm certain) and told me my card
had been declined. How humiliating! It was quite a while before
I could show my face there again, and when I did, that's all I
showed them. To avoid temptation, I left all forms of purchasing
power at home. Now, when I can't afford to buy, I have to settle
for being buy-curious.

It's not as simple as declaring you'll give up gratuitous shopping altogether. Shopping, the present-day expression of the urge
to hunt, is in our blood. Our hunting and gathering ancestors
survived quite nicely for about a million years. In fact, it was
only after they picked the store clean that they had to start
growing crops, which they then traded (or "shopped") for other

things they needed. There are significant moments in history that we owe to the premeditated exchange of money for goods. Marketplaces along the silk and spice routes became The Place to pick up news, technology, and gossip from around the world. Shopping is the reason that people living in the corn belt don't speak French (thank you, Thomas Jefferson!). When you shop, you awaken your DNA's most basic purpose.

So what's a girl with a declined credit card and wide-awake DNA to do? Why not start with a Bloody Mary? This one is very simple and will supply enough thrill of the chase to keep you out of the mall for good. Here's how:

* First, get out a glass. You won't be able to fit all the ingredients in a regular shot glass, so your best bet would be a tall shot glass, which holds anywhere from 2½ to 4 ounces. Yours may say something like "Amy's Bachelorette Party 1987," but it's probably the right size. If you can't find one, you can get by with a small 5- or 6-ounce juice glass. (See? You're hunting already.)

* Now, unwrap a package of beef ramen noodles and get out the seasoning packet.

    As far as the noodles go, you can do one of three things:
    1. make your next batch a double, using only the one seasoning packet. It will still taste great;
    2. add the orphaned noodles to a stir fry;
    3. serve them as a side dish with a little butter and garlic.

* Dissolve the contents of the packet in your glass, along with the tomato juice. Next on the list is the

vodka and tomato juice. These tend to be things you either have or you don't. If you fall into the "don't" category, hit up a friend or neighbor. Do not, whatever you do, go to the store. The store is just a big fluorescent-lit den of temptation. They lure you in with their big glossy displays, and before you can say "Paper, please," you've purchased thirty-seven things you don't need. Besides, it's really good to know where other Bloody Mary fans live. You could set up a whole Bloody network. (You didn't think you were the only one in this boat, did you?) Pour the tomato juice into your chosen glass.

* Here's where the hunt can get interesting. Some people keep their drive-thru condiments in a hidden corner of the fridge. Others toss them in a drawer. Your hot sauce hiding place could be in the pocket of the door of your car or even under the seat. If you come up dry in all of those places, keep looking. Those packets don't have an expiration date, so don't be afraid to look in pockets of the coat you haven't worn since Amy's bachelorette party. When you find the hot sauce, add as much as you want to the drink-in-progress. Stir everything together, then down the hatch it goes.

That's all there is to it! Let's recap what just happened. You saved some money, maybe made some friends, got some exercise, satisfied a primal urge, and had a delicious drink. You won't find a better return on investment in this economy.

There's Nothing Fun to Do This Weekend

Serves 1

I jigger vodka
I jigger dirty martini mixer
(Stirrings or Dirty Rose are both good)
I jigger Bloody Mary mix
Tabasco sauce, to taste
Several green olives, to serve

In a cocktail shaker, combine all the ingredients (minus the olives) with plenty of ice cubes. Shake until blended, and strain into a martini glass. Add the olives and serve. Sometimes all the fun you need is right under your nose.

Sec(retarie)s in the City.

et's face facts, girlie Q. You are in desperate need of new friends. All your current friends want to do, it seems, is go out to dinner or watch *Dancing with the Stars*. Am I overreacting? Not as much as you're overeating. Don't get me wrong; I adore food as much as anyone, and I never turn down a chance to scope out a new chef or a trendy new nightspot. I also enjoy cheap entertainment. But as the weather turns from abysmal to somewhat tolerable, aren't you beginning to crave activities that are more, well, active? You know what they say about variety. Well, it happens to be true.

Speaking of which, here's a unique new Bloody Mary to try. It has Spice of Life written all over it. After you've had one or two, I'll help you with a project that's guaranteed to change your life.

But first, the drink. It's a fun little hybrid of a dirty martini and a Bloody Mary. It takes no time at all to make or consume, so you won't miss out on a minute of the fun. It tastes like an uptown twist on a downtown flavor. Delicious when enjoyed separately but spectacular when mixed together. Think Li'l Kim and Michelle Obama trading clothes for the day. Or imagine the lovechild of Chris Rock and Judi Dench. If you choose not to serve it in a martini glass, it looks equally at home in a rocks glass over ice. Heck, serve it in a Tiffany champagne flute or a beer bong for all I care. The sky's the limit! You can't say that about very many drinks, now can you? Bloody Mary is the patron saint of versatility.

Now let's get back to your posse problem. Maybe instead of amassing a new group of think-outside-the-house friends, consider teaching your crowd how to shake things up a bit. They may be secretly wishing for a leader such as yourself to get the ball rolling. Below is a list of verbs (action words) and next to that is a list of places one could conceivably go in a decent-sized city. What you do is cut them all out and put them in two separate bowls—verbs in one, places in another. Close your eyes and choose one piece of paper out of each bowl. The group has to do whatever it says. Next time, someone else gets a turn to pick. Get the idea? Okay, I'll wait while you add your own ideas and cut up the lists.

Verbs	Places
skate	at the art museum
shop	in the park
dance	at a street market
ride	on public transit
climb	in a theater
watch	in a sports facility
play	at a day spa
learn	at a friend's house
hike	at the outlet mall
explore	in a nearby town

Did you and your friends find a few new things to try? Great! Don't forget to add your new favorite Bloody Mary to the list. After all, you've got to come home sometime, and you'll be thirsty from all the excitement. If your friends aren't quite on board yet, take heart. Go pioneering by yourself the first time. You'll make like-minded friends while you're there, and they're likely to turn you on to even more activity ideas. In turn, they'll want to know all about your interesting new Bloody Mary. The downside? Your couch is going to miss you.

It's Raining for the 47th Day in a Row

Serves 1

1 Tbsp. cayenne pepper
2 shots Absolut Peppar vodka
2 oz. Spicy Hot V8
2 oz. Clamato
1 pepperoncini, to serve
1 olive, to serve

Combine the first four ingredients in a cocktail shaker, strain, and pour over ice cubes in an Old Fashioned glass. Garnish with the pepperoncini and the olive, and serve. Dry yourself out with a little self-immolation.

*Drat! Storm clouds... I shaved
my legs for nothing!*

An afternoon of rain is romantic. A weekend of rain is disappointing. A solid week of rain is depressing. A month of rain is coma-inducing. By the middle of Month 2 of nothing but rain, you're trying to decide which puddle you can drown yourself in. Meteorologists in the Pacific Northwest think they're being cute because they know about a hundred different names for rain. Like if they call it something clever, it won't be as wet. "On the weather map, we see tomorrow's forecast calling for drizzle, followed by two or three days of liquid sunshine. Later in the week you can expect some showers, with precipitation likely in the higher elevations. Right now we've got sprinkles developing into a steady cloudburst by morning. Back to you, Ted."

They're not fooling me. I was born in the Northwest, and I have the webbed feet to prove it. I know it's gonna rain (mist, downpour, gulleywash) from Columbus Day until Mother's Day. That doesn't change the fact that it sucks. Apart from packing up whatever's still dry and moving south for the fall, winter, and spring, there's only one thing to do: perform a ceremonial Enough-With-The-Rain-Already Dance. To do this, we are going to borrow from a few different indigenous customs that have been practiced in the shamanistic arts for centuries by shamans who know what they're talking about.

1. Clear the ceremonial space of large pieces of furniture, breakable knick-knacks, and debris on the floor.

2. The Zuni tradition dictates that dancers be barefoot; men dance nude except for a kilt, while women are supposed to be wrapped in shawls from noggin to knees. (Hey, I didn't make the rules. Just do it.)

3. Prepare the Bloody Mary in the shaker as described above.

4. Hop around in circles, shaking the drink vigorously. Be sure you are hopping counter-clockwise, otherwise you will bring more rain. Chant "Enough with the Rain Already!" once for each day it has been raining. If you choose not to chant, you can do what the Hopi tribe does and dance around with a venomous snake in your mouth. (Again, I don't make the rules.)

5. Next, we will perform an ancient Sioux custom. Put the shaker down in the middle of the floor. Make four more hoppy circles around the shaker and continue to chant (unless of course you decided to use the snake method.) Throw yourself down on the floor, then drink the contents of the

shaker. There is some serious spice happening here, so go slow.

Now, take a look out the window. Did it stop raining? Or is the heat wave only in your mouth?

I Haven't Had a Cold This Bad in Years

Serves 4

I cup freshly squeezed orange juice
I cup extra spicy Bloody Mary mix
1/2 cup freshly squeezed lime juice
3 tsp. grenadine
Dash of chili powder
Pinch of salt
Freshly ground black pepper, to taste
Tequila, to serve

Combine all ingredients (except the tequila) in a glass pitcher. Add ice cubes and stir well. Serve chilled in highball glasses as a chaser alongside shots of room-temperature tequila. These are the best kind of shots—no needles!

I'm pretty sure I'm not contagious anymore…
Hello? Where did everybody go?

Nowadays, there's a drug for every problem under the sun. There are drugs to regulate your bodily functions. There are drugs to regulate how you feel about your bodily functions. There are drugs that help all your other drugs work better. There are drugs to deal with the side effects of other drugs. Do you ever read the fine print? "This medicine has been proven to control sugar cravings in middle-aged laboratory animals, but it is also known to cause hallucinations, rashes, diarrhea, global aphasia, impotence, liquification of striated muscle, and episodes of bleeding from the eyes. Ask your doctor if Sugargonazine is right for you."

Feed a cold, starve a fever. That's what my mother always said, and no doubt her mother did too. Now that I'm a mom (with internet access, no less), I can tell you exactly what to feed your cold to get you back on your feet fast. And without pills! Each ingredient in this Bloody Mary promotes good health, increases your alertness, brightens your mood, and gives you energy. Let me break them down for you.

* **Bloody Mary mix:** Many brands boast 170 percent vitamin C and 60 percent RDA of vitamin A, otherwise known as the anti-infection vitamin. Check your labels for the highest nutritional rating.

* **Orange juice / lime juice:** Also packed with vitamin C, the juice from citrus fruits offers a well-documented way to build up your immune system. It can help you fend off a bug to begin with, or it can help you fight one if you're already sick. Orange juice also soothes a sore throat and thins the consistency of mucus.

* **Grenadine:** This is a thick, sweet syrup made from pomegranates and red currants. The medicinal value of both these fruits has been circulating for thousands of years. They act as powerful antioxidants to help repair cells and put up your body's best defense.

* **Chili powder:** It's no coincidence that your nose runs whenever you eat spicy food. Capsaicin, which, you may recall, is what makes a chili pepper taste, well, peppery, stimulates secretions that help clear mucus from your lungs and nose. Capsaicin also plays a role in pain relief and has been proven to help boost your immune system.

* **Salt:** Okay, you got me there. Other than traces of iodine in table salt, which supports thyroid

function, there is no evidence that salt is good for treating a head cold.

* **Black pepper:** When your nose is so stuffy that you can't taste much, black pepper can make food more palatable. It also works as an antioxidant, and counteracts the buildup of intestinal gas. In sufficient quantities, it aids your body's ability to sweat out harmful toxins.

* **Tequila:** Many of the health benefits of tequila have nothing to do with the upper respiratory tract, but I'll list them here anyway. It helps raise good cholesterol and lowers bad cholesterol. It can reduce your risk of getting dementia. When consumed after a meal, it aids digestion. And who can argue with its sleep-inducing or mood-elevating properties?

You look like you're starting to feel better. Open the window for a little fresh air. Take a warm bath. Then take two Bloody Marys, and call me in the morning.

My moms, before I was a twinkle in their eyes.

Epilogue

As a four-year-old playing with my dolls, I acted out the role of Mommy. That mostly consisted of feeding them, changing their diapers, and tucking them into bed. I sang them the same songs my mommy sang to me. I gave them birthday parties and haircuts. As mommies go, I was a natural. My babies never cried, and they did everything I told them to. Being a mommy was easy, and a mommy was all I wanted to be from then on.

A few years later, I graduated to playing with Barbies. Barbie and Ken were too busy to have babies. They played tennis, drove around in Jeeps and convertibles, hung out on the beach and at the dog park, went on glamorous dates, and dabbled in different careers. They had friends, and a niece as I recall, but no children of their own. Come to think of it, they didn't have parents, either. So that's how they got away with living in the same Dream House together. And in the sixties, no less. Even Rob and Laura Petrie slept in twin beds on *The Dick Van Dyke Show*, and they were not only married but had a child to boot. That might have been the point in my life when the whole mommy-worship thing began to weaken around the edges. Barbie sure seemed to be having an awful lot of family-sold-separately fun.

Then I became a teenager. Honestly, I can't figure out how my mother got so stupid so quickly. I mean, suddenly she just didn't understand me at all. She had unwanted opinions about my friends, my clothes, my grades, my complexion, my curfew... Who did she think she was? And why did my friends all think she was so cool? Okay, yes, she decorated our gorgeous house

I Think I'm Turning into My Mother

Serves 1

> 1 jigger citrus vodka
> 1 jigger pepper vodka
> Dash of Worcestershire sauce
> Salt and black pepper, to taste
> Tabasco sauce, to taste
> 6 oz. Bloody Mary mix
> 1/2 lime, cut into 2 wedges

Fill a highball glass with cubed or crushed ice. Add all the ingredients except the lime, and stir well. Squeeze the juice of 1 lime quarter into the drink, discard, and use the other one as a garnish.

all by herself, had excellent taste in fashion and books, and was generous to a fault. But they didn't have to live with her, doing my laundry, waiting up for me...it was totally gross. I didn't ever want to have kids; but if I did, I was Never Going to Treat Them This Way.

Ten years and two babies later, my mom and I were best friends again. For the first time, I saw that moms have to be two-dimensional to (a) survive and (b) do their job. That sweet, sunny disposition is fine when all is going smoothly, but you have to be ready to bust out some firepower when the situation warrants it. And through good times and bad, keep your backbone straight but maintain the ability to laugh at yourself. My mom was good at that. She knew how to keep it all in balance—a feat that's taken me twenty-five years and counting to get right.

This Bloody Mary gets it right the first time. With two kinds of vodka, it gives you all the flavor you could ask for and twice the kick. A little Worcestershire sauce for structure, a little lime for cheerfulness, a little seasoning for *hutzpah*. How can you go wrong? The weird thing is, the more of it I put in my mouth, the more Mom Wisdom comes out. Who can forget these classics?

* "If (insert friend's name here) jumped off a cliff, would you?"

* "Put that down; you don't know where it's been."

* "Don't make that face; it will freeze that way."

* "I'll give you something to cry about."

* "You can't have dessert until you clean your plate."

* "Where do you think you're going dressed like that?"

＊ "Because I said so."

＊ "Can we have *no* nice things?"

Wow. All of a sudden I want a Bloody Mary. And I want to give my mom a hug. And apologize to my daughter. All you moms out there, I salute you. What we're doing is far from easy, and sometimes not very much fun. But I wouldn't trade any of it for Barbie's lifestyle if you handed it to me on a pink plastic platter.

Bottoms up, my Bloody Mary soulmate! Bottoms up...

Recipe References

Actually, I'm More of a Ski Lodge Bum (p. 134)—A dazzling little recipe from www.cdkitchen.com. Thanks, ladies!

All I Need Is Comfort Food and a Little "Me" Time (p. 168)— www.cdkitchen.com again.

Blondes May Have More Fun, But Brunettes Have Better Fun (p. 178)—You can thank Suzanne Mauget of Bogart's American Grill in Raleigh, North Carolina, for this one. They're at 510 Glenwood Ave.

Go Packers (p. 68)—Donated by Dave and Cindy Hyde, the other cutest couple I know (besides Tom and me).

Good Help Is So Hard to Find (p. 172)—My recipe, after lots of failed experiments and muffled cursing.

He Called Out My Sister's Name in Bed (p. 74)—From Salvador Molly's in Portland, Oregon, with permission from Marie Dietrich.

Hos Before Bros (p. 116)—I heard about this from bartender friends and had to try it for myself.

I Can't Manage My Money If I Don't Have Any (p. 196)— Frank Kelly Rich gave me this little gem. He's from *Modern Drunkard Magazine*.

I Haven't Had a Cold This Bad in Years (p. 208)—This is from an article by Dee Hitch of the *Mercer Island Reporter*, dated September 15, 2005.

I Know We Just Met, But I Want to Have Your Babies (p. 54)—From answers@yahoo.com.

I Landed the Account, Bitchez (p. 24)—My own creation.

I Need a Hobby Now That the Kids Have Left Home (p. 184) — Given to me by Ezra Johnson-Greenough right after his OCD support group meeting.

I Never Got to Go Backpacking Through Europe (p. 142) — By Karen Hochman, from www.thenibble.com, December 2005.

I Oughta Put a Big Carbon Footprint Right On Your Face, You SUV-Driving, Animal-Eating, Plastic-Wrapped, High-Fructose Son of a Bitch (p. 88) — Also from www.cdkitchen. com.

I Really Hope I Fit In at This New Country Club (p. 62) — Used by permission from www.cdkitchen.com. (Oh, now they're just showing off.)

I Spent Three Months in Palm Desert One Weekend (p. 158) — This is my hybrid of all the Bloody Mary granita recipes that came my way.

I Think I'm Turning into My Mother (p. 214) — I don't remember where this one came from, so I'll say it's mine. You can't sue me because I don't have any money.

I Want This Promotion So Bad I Can Taste It (p. 58) — Courtesy of yours truly.

If You Think I'm Paying for This Haircut, You're Sadly Mistaken (p. 82) — My recipe, with my opinions thrown in for free.

It Took Me All Friggin' Weekend, But I Finally Got the Grout Clean (p. 8) — I started with a recipe by NCMysteryshopper@ yahoo.com, then I played around with it a little bit.

It's My Birthday and I Want Breakfast in Bed (p. 100) — Courtesy of Tori Harms at McCormick & Schmick's.

It's Not You, It's Me (p. 192) — Inspired by the wonderful Kara

Newman, author of *Spice and Ice*. I have a huge girl-crush on this woman.

It's Raining for the 47th Day in a Row (p. 204)—Another one of my recipes. It's a gift.

I've Decided to Go Back to College (p. 138)—An experiment that turned out rather well, if I do say so myself.

Let Me Be the First to Welcome You to the Neighborhood (Petiot's Original Bloody Mary) (p. 2)—Karen Hochman, www. thenibble.com, December 2005. Her boss said I could have it.

Maybe They Won't Notice I Burned the Steaks (p. 36)—Based on www.wikihow.com/Make-A-Michelada, but the rimming mixture is mine.

My Daughter's New Boyfriend Isn't an Asswipe (p. 28)—Also my own.

My High School Reunion is Five Pounds and Two Weeks Away (p. 112)—Used by permission from Alex Lieber of www. ediets.com.

My Kids Found My "Private Drawer" (p. 92)—Just a little something I threw together.

My Tax Refund Just Bought Me a Week in Cabo (p. 130)—I came up with this one during a lightning storm.

Remind Me Why I'm Going Skydiving Tomorrow (p. 46)— Loosely based on "The Gunsmith" at Johnny Utah's (25 W. 51st Street, New York). What a crazy night…

Tell Us Again How He Proposed (Hemingway's Perfect Bloody Mary) (p. 20)—From a letter to Bernard Peyton signed April 5, 1947, by Ernest Hemingway; referenced in *The Bloody Mary*, by Christopher B. O'Hara, The Lyons Press, 1999, and about two hundred other places on the web.

The More Resentment I Release, the More Love I Can Express (p. 120)—This is an old family standby, popular on deep-sea fishing trips.

The Pregnancy Test Was Negative (p. 16)—This one taught me that you shouldn't eavesdrop unless you are prepared to take precise notes. I had to start over from scratch.

The Way to a Man's Heart Is Through His Stomach, But That's Not Where I'm Headed (p. 40)—I claim this one.

There's Nothing Fun to Do This Weekend (p. 200)—My creation. If you can't beat 'em, join 'em.

They Told Me It Was a Costume Party (p. 78)—The result of my quest to create a Red Bull Bloody Mary. It didn't work, but this one did.

This Is My First Really Healthy Relationship (p. 108)—Contributed by Bev Fagan at a weak moment.

This Outfit and I Deserve a Night On the Town (p. 104)—From Troy Itami of Buffalo Gap, 6835 SW Macadam Avenue, Portland, Oregon.

Tonight's Our Anniversary and My Mom's Watching the Kids (p. 12)—My own recipe but inspired by one provided by www.jager.com.

We Need a Bigger Garage (p. 164)—Just like Mama used to make. Seriously.

We Should Go to Hawaii More Often (p. 146)—This is my riff on the Thai Bloody Mary at Alfa, 1709 Walnut Street, Philadelphia, Pennsylvania. Smooches to Joe for being a great sport.

What a Perfect Day for a Picnic (p. 150)—From the (in)famous Florida Room, 435 N. Killingsworth, Portland, Oregon, and its mayor, Patty Earley.

What's the Guatemalan Phrase for "Please Untie Me" (p. 154) —
My husband dreamed this one up while I googled Guatemala.

When I Win the Lottery, I'm Quitting This Crappy Job (p. 50) —
This one's mine, too.

About the Author

J udy Bennett has been called "screamingly funny" and "the Erma Bombeck of booze." She is a native of Portland, Oregon, and her hobbies include exploring new or underappreciated venues for food, drink, shopping, art, and culture. When she isn't behind the bar, she is most likely: a) organizing her 112-pair shoe collection; b) selling vintage resort wear on her web site, www. thousandislanddressing.net; c) performing burlesque under her stage name, Nadia Nice; or d) teaching wellness seminars for those who lead crazy, busy, boozy lives like hers. In her personal life, she has been happily married nine times to the same fabulous man. Some of her Bloody Mary recipes can be found in *Chili Pepper Magazine* and *Grocery Gardening*, by Jean Ann Van Krevelen, and she is also the author of *If You're Old and You Know It, Clap Your Hands: How to Grow Old—And Love It.*